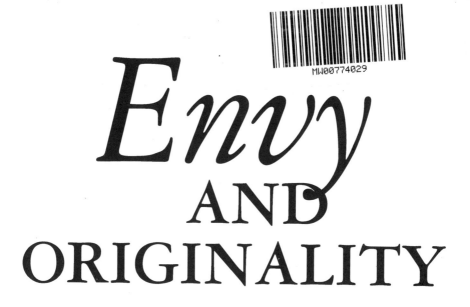

Envy AND ORIGINALITY

BY
ADRIAN VAN KAAM

REVISED AND EDITED BY
SUSAN MUTO

Epiphany Books
Pittsburgh, Pennsylvania

Envy and Originality

Epiphany Books
An Imprint of Epiphany Association
820 Crane Avenue
Pittsburgh, PA 15216
www.epiphanyassociation.org

ISBN: 1880982471
ISBN 13: 9781880982471
Library of Congress Catalog No. 2011938114
Epiphany Association, Pittsburgh, PA

SELECTED WORKS BY ADRIAN VAN KAAM

Life Journey of the Joyful Man of God:
The Autobiographical Memoirs of Adrian van Kaam

Religion and Personality
Spirituality and the Gentle Life
The Transcendent Self

Formative Spirituality Series
Fundamental Formation
Human Formation
Formation of the Human Heart
Scientific Formation
Traditional Formation
Transcendent Formation
Transcendence Therapy

SELECTED WORKS CO-AUTHORED WITH SUSAN MUTO

Am I Living a Spiritual Life?
Divine Guidance
The Power of Appreciation

Formation Theology Series
Foundations of Christian Formation
Christian Articulation of the Mystery
Formation of the Christian Heart
Living Our Christian Faith and Formation Traditions

CONTENTS

Contents

Preface

Adrian van Kaam's book, *Envy and Originality*, was first published by Doubleday in 1972. In that same year, he articulated several of its themes in terms of the Christian formation tradition in his book, *On Being Yourself*, a Dimension Books publication. The latter publisher acquired the rights to reissue *Envy and Originality* in paperback in 1985 under a new title, *Living Creatively*.

Now this new version of *Envy and Originality* returns the book to its original title and brings its seminal thinking up to date with the science, anthropology, and theology of formation.

The themes it highlights, notably patterns of envy, escalating tactics of envy, envy in childhood, approaching adult living, and dwelling and original living, make this book essential reading for anyone pursuing fidelity to their original call in today's world.

Such core concepts in the van Kaamian theory of personality point to the basic necessity of respect for one's own and others' original life call and the motivations stemming from it. The author intends that his reflections be seen as passionate appeals for the just treatment of people hemmed in by envy and oppression in any leveling society or community.

Original people feel at times like lonely voices crying in the wilderness. They are aware of such obvious signs of social injustice as racism as well as far deeper forms of intolerance committed against the congeniality rights of countless people in all segments of the world population.

As the editor of this revised edition of *Envy and Originality*, I echo Adrian van Kaam's conviction that we must commit ourselves to honor our dignity as children of God and recommit ourselves to the struggle to uphold originality on every level of society. May this book be a tribute to his and our lifelong efforts to realize this Christian formation ideal.

Susan Muto, Ph.D., Dean
Epiphany Academy of Formative Spirituality
Pittsburgh, Pennsylvania

Acknowledgments

I am deeply grateful to the staff of our Epiphany Academy of Formative Spirituality for aiding my editorial efforts—to Vicki Bittner for diligent retypes of the manuscript; to Mary Lou Perez for solving production issues; to our publishers for their creative support; and, of course, to our Board of Directors for their encouragement and financial enabling of this project. As we have discovered time and again, Adrian van Kaam's thinking was always ahead of its time. His concepts are as fresh and vivid today as when he first pondered the unbelievable attacks the sin of envy levels against any sign of originality. No one who ponders his words and applies them to daily life will ever forget his wise and freeing counsel. To his living memory and his innovative concepts, we respond with heartfelt gratitude.

This new edition of his groundbreaking work on the dynamics of envy, original living, and envious comparison has been revised and edited to honor the memory of my colleague, mentor, and friend, Rev. Adrian van Kaam, CSSp, PhD (1920-2007).

Chapter One
Envy of Originality

During the infamous Dutch Hunger Winter of 1944-1945, I had to flee from my home city, The Hague, to find a hiding place in the small farming and fishing village of Nieuwkoop. The leader of the resistance there was a mailman, a daring and cunning person, who knew how to outwit the enemy. The few of us who were aware of his feats of courage spoke of him with awe. Peter, it seems, had always been a man of original force and integrity, but it took a terrible war to reveal his gifts in a way no one had foreseen. Was Peter an original man before the war? Would his originality have come to the fore without the war?

Originality is like a unique mark we receive at birth. It is our latent ability to be ourselves in our own way. We may or may not be faithful to that power in us. Peter always seemed to have been himself, as a boy in school, as a mailman, as a young husband and father. Now he was himself as a leader of the resistance. He was still the same Peter, but he displayed his gifts in a new light.

Whether or not we allow our uniqueness to become a source of growth is a choice we have to make. We can then ask ourselves what form our originality will take. The answer at any given moment of life has a lot to do with the situations in which we find ourselves. Special occasions invite us to be our unique self in ways we might not have foreseen.

Peter's whole life could have been spent taking care of his family and carrying the mail. He would have accepted these tasks in his own way and been good at them. As a man faithful to his originality, he would have become as unique a person as possible in service of others. Then the war came. It put Peter in an unexpected position. He responded to this new challenge as he had done to the demands of daily life before the German

1

occupation. He was simply himself, only now as a leader in the resistance. This situation, however, brought other dimensions of his originality to the fore. It compelled him to develop new skills and attitudes. These did not grow in isolation from his initial originality; rather, they expanded his ability to be himself and to exercise his "can do" attitude. During the war and in many ways after it, Peter was able to realize his potential in a different and more expanded fashion than before this nightmare of usurped freedom.

INITIAL AND HISTORICAL ORIGINALITY

Our history has a lot to do with what our originality will be like. We could call this originality, as it manifests itself at certain moments of our life, historical as distinct from our initial originality, which refers to the possibility of being who we most deeply are in a way that conforms to the marks of uniqueness we receive as our birthright. In the beginning this gift is a mere possibility. Only history will record what we do with it, whether we bury this birthright or let it come to life, whether we develop our originality in response to the challenges we must confront or forfeit it in fear.

I had relatives like Peter—enterprising businessmen, social-minded and philanthropic. In a few generations they worked themselves up from blue collar laborers to captains of industry, who allowed their gifts to expand in response to the economic situations they faced in their lives. Other members of my own and Peter's family were not like that at all, though this dissimilarity did not determine their character formation. The question is: how faithful were they to their own gifts? Reaching this answer is the work of a lifetime, but in my opinion Peter had made a good start.

We do not know immediately what the best course of action is for us, but we do become aware of certain likes and dislikes we cannot easily shake. However much we may try to resist them, they return to our conscious- ness again and again. To what kind of life these inclinations point we may not yet know. Only in the course of living may we discover which styles of being and doing make it possible for us to be faithful to our original gifts and which make it more difficult for us to remain true to ourselves.

For another friend of mine, it became clear that he could not follow in the footsteps of his father and his uncles and be a banker or the president of a company. He found himself interested in ranching and in writing novels. Being faithful to his initial originality was not going to make for a smooth ride. It first revealed itself to him in leanings and feelings that were indefinite and confusing. Why was he so different from his other siblings and cousins? He tried to ignore these spontaneous inclinations. Some of them flared up and then disappeared. They proved to be only momentary impulses or fleeting impressions. Others returned tenaciously. They were indicators of what were to be true and lasting gifts of his. He began to discover that he could be faithful to himself in a variety of educational settings, provided he made the business courses he had to take secondary to his love for literature. Somewhere along the line of his upbringing, he decided that no role he was supposed to play could compel him to betray who he was. To be sure, certain experiences gave him more scope than others to pursue his own gifts, including spending his summer vacations on a working ranch and enrolling for several writing seminars. These freely chosen expressions of his originality encouraged him to affirm and deepen his unique-communal life call. As a result, initially vague inclinations became more definite. He began to feel that he could express himself as a speaker to his listeners and as a writer to his readers. He trusted his originality to shape his history. There was no denying that he felt more competent as a rancher than a captain of industry, more true to himself as a novelist than an investment banker.

To give a definite direction to my spontaneous inclinations marks the beginning of original living in my everyday situation. Important as this first orientation is, it is not enough. Initial insights into my God-given destiny and the feelings that accompany them need to be translated into action. If originality and my original calling are to be the guiding principles of my daily life, I need to discern more than what road I should take or what role I should play among the many possible ones offered to me. I must walk that road and play that role with such fidelity that what was once only an inclination now becomes a persistent and effective course of action.

It was not enough for my friend to opt on one or the other occasion to be a rancher and a novelist. He had to make this intention an enduring option. He had to work to embody it consistently. Only then could these gifts come to full flowering in detailed and particular ways. Only then could the originality that was a possibility became a reality. The insight and drive to be his best self in service of others had to be raised to a higher plane: from wish fulfillment to constant effective willing.

ORIGINALITY AND SELF-MOTIVATION

My initial originality must be transformed into a concrete plan of action that shapes my life realistically. This operational originality then becomes a driving force within me. Under its guiding light, seemingly scattered insights and inspirations begin to be integrated at the core of my emerging character and personhood. Central to my vocation and the advocations that sustain it is the mysterious calling that guides my life from birth to death. The course of action it initiates becomes the basis of my future motivations and decisions. The option to be faithful to my life call is not an incidental event like deciding what car to drive or where to buy a home. This option refers to a lasting orientation that moves me from within as distinct from passing motives to do this or that, especially when others try to convince me that I should pursue a certain plan or project whether it is what the mystery wants for me or not. Some suggestions more than others may help me to discern my life direction, but I must find a way to make them my own.

Self-motivation of this sort shapes my life continuously. It enables me to internalize and transform the new options offered to me by the slow but sure unveiling of my call. In the process of its appropriation, one or the other opening may become an avenue to the ongoing revelation of God's providential plan for my life.

My friend told me about a well-meaning relative of his who challenged his choice of ranching by saying that what really moved him to go West was that it was the easiest way out of the pressures of business. My friend pondered the validity of this critique, but it was not enough to convince him to change the course to which his calling had led him so far. One does not put one's future on the line simply because a certain kind of life is seen by outsiders to be easier than another. Ranching may seem to be less demanding than banking, but my friend knew he would need every business skill he had acquired to succeed in land purchases, to hire good hands to manage the livestock, and to raise his children in remote country settings.

My friend had to consider more than once what motivated him to choose this original course of action. It would have been a lot easier for him to assent to the avocations proposed by his family. He had to balance the hardships of ranching against the advantages he could have had in the business world, but no rationale made sense in the light of the person he was. Ease of operations was not a good enough motive for him. It did not meet the criterion of personal meaning, which alone could bring him in contact with the blessings and burdens of being at the same time a rancher and a writer. This inner direction went beyond external "motivation" to internal "self-motivation." It became a matter of the heart. My friend could have falsified his life under family pressure. He might have allowed himself to be motivated to serve society solely by leadership in the business world. The familial credentials were impeccable. He saw what security and success they had produced for his relatives and their employees. It was tempting to silence the voice of inner self-motivation and follow in their footsteps. The trouble was their love for the business world would have been alien to the motives urging him to another way of life. He would operate under the demands of others and end up a stranger to himself. Countless people fall into this trap. The motivation to join the family firm would have secured him a respected position but diminished his pursuit of happiness. He would have succeeded as a banker but living such a borrowed life might have destroyed him as a person.

SELF-MOTIVATION AND CULTURAL MOTIVES

The initial originality, bestowed on us already at birth, remains a possibility that can only be realized when we begin to transform our latent uniqueness into an operational set of goals that enable us to be and become our true self. Self-motivation in tune with our initial originality enables this transformation to take place. The seed for such motivation not only implants itself in us initially; it also comes to us from the culture in which we live. A precautionary note alerts us to the fact that we should never adopt blindly any motivation we see operable there; rather cultural motivations should become ours according to the following criteria.

First, we must select those which are as compatible as possible with our self-motivations. While we appreciate motives that seem to be suitable for others, we ought not to make them the shaping forces in our own life. For example, I may be an avid supporter of the symphony and of its director's original musical creations without feeling of lesser value because I am neither a musician nor a composer.

Secondly, we must find ways to embody chosen cultural motivations until such time as they become our own. We must root them in the rich soil of our uniqueness and allow them to be pervaded by our originality. Usually this link occurs spontaneously, on the condition that we do not halt the process by imitating others who may be at a different place than we are. The cultural motivations we appropriate may have much in common with others, but still we live them in a different way. Every motivation undergoes a subtle transformation when it becomes an instrument of our originality.

My friend wanted to be a novelist for as long as he could remember. He happened to discover that ranching would be compatible with this call. His self-motivation to be a writer would have been impossible without an already existing cultural motivation to have a place of his own under, in his words, "the open sky." He saw the value of living in the kind of climate that motivates a person to write. Encapsulation in the world of business was for him counterproductive to the adventurous novels he dreamed of composing. Writing them and living as a rancher melded together in a task-oriented rhythm of labor and leisure that enabled him to incarnate his initial originality.

This cultural motivation easily became his own because he permeated it with a sense of his inmost transcendent identity. He was at home with his uniqueness. His novels told a good story where characters expressed feelings and concerns that found points of resonance in the life world of his readers. My friend kept close to his heart the motivation to live in fidelity to his call to be a writer, not in blind conformity to a set pattern, but in the way best suited to his originality. In short, he found harmony between his self-motivation and the motives sustaining it in his culture.

INVENTIVENESS AND ORIGINALITY

When we hear the word "originality," we may not think about people who live their lives in a rather modest and inconspicuous way. Our first thought is that original persons must be inventive people who, for example, design new cars, set fashion trends, and devise manufacturing methods unknown in the past. Inventiveness of this sort may or may not be rooted in personal originality. It is rather obvious that we cannot tell much about the personality of an inventor from what he or she invents. The light bulb does not give us much insight into the inner life of Thomas Edison. Inventors may be so fascinated by their claim to fame that other facets of their formation field pale in comparison. They may be inventive as promoters of products but unoriginal as persons. The opposite is also true. One may live an original life in the personal sense without being inventive at all.

The kind of inventiveness that insures profit and production may attract praise in a particular culture. Inventiveness may be fostered while inner living remains frowned upon. Inventors may be the recipients of social benefits, whether or not they manifest any originality as human beings. Conformity to the culture may become a higher motivation than congeniality with one's true call. Such cultural motivations may override the inner claims to self-motivation that enhance one's quality of life and make original experiences possible.

When I see how successful inventive types are, I may envy their fame and fortune. In attempting to be like them, I may show off ideas, attitudes, and mannerisms that are not really my own. I merely imitate what seems to look original. My words and deeds do not flow from the inner stream of my integrity. They express a make-believe originality that deforms me as a person. I am no longer moved by the awareness of who I should be. All that motivates me is my desire to create a public image of inventive originality so that I, too, may amass the popularity, possessions, and powers others put on the highest rung of the ladder of success.

Such outer motives eat away at my inner motivational life like corrosive acid. They put at risk the liberating sense of self-motivation. Once it erodes almost to the point of absence, my originality may be in danger of being permanently suppressed. Selfhood or human originality is not a gift we can take for granted; it needs to be nurtured daily. An "original person" is a "self-motivated" soul. The moment self-motivation weakens, so does our deepest identity, but all is not lost. If we have the courage to reclaim our originality, we can recover. No longer do we mistake our originality for the quest to be inventive or creative in an outward manner only. To foster original living inwardly we must be wise enough to avoid the pitfalls of either blind imitation out of envy or stubborn rebellion out of egocentric pride. We must remember that we can be original inwardly without being outwardly different. Similarly, we can be outwardly different without being inwardly original. As original persons, we do not need to invent new techniques for time management or display unusual traits. Ours may be the most ordinary of lives, not much different from that of others in our environment. Yet our originality shines through not because of *what* we do but because of the *way* we do it, not because of the possessions we *have* but because of the way we *live*.

REACHING SELF-MOTIVATION

What is the reason why our initial originality may remain dormant? What causes us not to actualize our inmost personhood through self-motivation?

Of all people, a cab driver I once met seemed to know the answers. He was a cheerful fellow, who loved his job and enjoyed picking up regular passengers like me. After we got more acquainted he told me he was thinking of upgrading his cab, revising his work schedule so he could spend a few more weekends with his family while trying to serve his customers as efficiently as ever. Knowing I was a professor of psychology, he asked if I'd like to hear more of his philosophy of life. I nodded my assent and he said: "I've been driving a cab for twenty years now. I love it! I could have had other better paying jobs, but this is the one I like the best. It's a good fit for the kind of guy I am. You know why I'm happy? Because I'm doing what I feel gives me the freedom to earn a living by being my own boss. I don't compare myself with guys who make their money by other means. What's the use of envying anyone? People who act like that won't be happy for long."

This street-wise cab driver was a good teacher. Week by week, thanks to our appointed times, he told me many more anecdotes about himself and his business plan. What struck me most was his remark that those who persist in comparing themselves to others cannot be happy. This inclination to size ourselves up in relation to others' success is so customary today, we hardly notice it. Why does this tendency make us less content? A few examples may shed light on the problem of comparison in our culture.

Jane is anxious to know whether the dress she is wearing will be as stylish as her girlfriend's is. John's secret love for poetry makes him question his masculinity. To show what a real man he is, he forces himself to play longer rounds of golf than the other guys, to down several drinks at the bar, and to drive as fast as he can. Every employee in Ed's company compares himself with everyone in middle management, wondering who got what bonus or what his chances of promotion are or how best to cozy up to the boss.

These examples alert us to the fact that we can compare ourselves with others only in those aspects of life that are comparable to begin with, including, for example, style of dress, driving skills, salary, promotion, or favor with one's boss. None of these points tell us who a person really is, only what he or she *has*.

We cannot tell what is unique about a person from the house he or she can afford, from the money he makes or from her adroitness at bridge or golf. These talents tell us something about their technical skill or their business acumen, but they leave us in the dark about what makes them who they most deeply are. In what way are they different from anyone who lived before them or will live after them? Are they fulfilling or forfeiting their temporal and eternal destiny?

9

To compare without envy is to look for what is alike in us or for what differs in some degree while still remaining basically appreciative of our own and others' uniqueness. We both make money, but the amount may differ. We both wear business suits, but their design and texture are distinctive. We both play golf, but our skill may vary. Our uniqueness is in essence incomparable. The word itself means one of a kind. To meet a person in his or her uniqueness is to meet them in that dimension where he or she cannot be compared with others. Habits of comparison prevent us from both appreciating ourselves and coming to know and admire others personally. We substitute for genuine encounter a subtle process of quantification and elimination. We abstract from the persons we meet a few superficial facets that can easily be compared and then we let these partial points stand for the person as a whole.

Meet Mr. Johnson. What a great guy! He makes money hand over fist. He drinks like a fish, sleeps like a bear, and has a house worth half a million. Not one of these attributes, be they good or bad, familiarizes us with who Mr. Johnson really is. We know only where he stands in comparison to other highly paid executives with an enviable capacity for hard drinking and sound sleeping. What is worse, we may be inclined to rate our own worth on the same scale. We may feel great when our friends declare that it looks as if we can out-drink, out-sleep and out-distance Mr. Johnson!

The fatal flaw in this habit of envious comparison is that it reduces people to collections of quantifiable characteristics. We do not value one another for the original selves we are but for attributes that do not necessarily tell us anything about our uniqueness as human beings. We do not meet ourselves or others as persons. We reduce what we see to mismatched sets of measurable statistics. We have no time for honest pondering beyond a category like who owns that or who lives where. We ignore deeper questions and poke fun at people who honor perennial values. We want to level the playing field around everyone we meet. No one is allowed to stand out as too original. All are fitted into the measurable and comparable frames of reference set up by the anonymous masters of public opinion.

Due to the influence of the media, to a heightened emphasis on peer group conformity, and to the fear of rising above the crowd, there may be more pressure on us to reduce the population to levels of conformity unknown in other times and cultures. One underlying reason for the upsurge of the leveling mentality may be the emphasis on one of our rational functions: that of abstraction. It enables us to abstract from persons all that is unique to them, resulting in our ability to retain only what makes them comparable to others.

This abstract function of thought has its purpose. It contributes to the smooth organization of masses of people. By analyzing their comparative skills and measuring their rate of output, one can find ways to compete in the marketplace and to establish scales of expected outcomes. Promotion in any commercial enterprise depends on our competitive edge and on our rate of production, on our pleasing the public, and often on our doing what is politically correct. We are trained to do whatever it takes to reach previously defined goals and to try to outdo our competitors. An organization on track to succeed has to make sure it gets the best out of its employees. The higher the output, the more they stand to reap monetary rewards.

From the perspective of these measurable dimensions of reality, the art and discipline of abstraction appears to be essential. Unfortunately, in this world of competition and comparison, little or no attention may be paid to what is unique about people, including the depth of their spiritual life and their sense of service to others. The same dynamics of abstraction and comparison can slip into the life of a church. Interest begins to be centered on how active the congregation is in recruiting new members. How much they put in the collection basket takes precedence over their life of prayer and intimacy with the Lord. Publishing a list of who donated what in the bulletin may unwittingly cause the members to compare themselves with others to see who stands where on the scale of contributions.

While principles of abstraction and comparison shed light on certain functions in the secular world, they have a shadow side. Those who live in envious comparison lack the serenity of self-acceptance. They suffer from the need to put others in their place—to label them as leftist, rightist, or middle of the road; to mock any profession that is out of the mainstream; to label those who are for or against them. This leveling and labeling mentality brings many otherwise exploratory conversations to a standstill. One feels on the defensive or reduced to silence. No one wants to be just a representative of some abstract category without at least a semblance of acceptance on the basis of one's inner worth.

Labels are like the blades of scythes ready to level anyone who stands out as unusual. In the case of original persons, they are not easy to stick on. Incomparable types are a nuisance in climates polluted by envy. They had better hide their originality or suffer the consequences. The more we persist in comparing ourselves with one another, the unhappier we become. Is there any solution to this deformative disposition?

One step toward changing it starts when we admit that success as defined by the yardstick of societal pressures is a precarious measure of our worth. The criteria I apply to others boomerangs on me. I become the object of similar estimates guaranteed to confuse my real worth with what society says is commendable. I become anxious about what I look like in public. I am no longer carefree. I lose my sense of self-possession. I repress my call-appreciation.

The secret longing that stays with me like a haunting refrain is to be valued for who I am, not merely for what I do or how well I perform. The older I get the more I know that someone will outdo me no matter how many promotions I've received. How long can I live under the stress of having to look better than others on the job, in the neighborhood or at my church? It pains me to have to hide my originality because people resent the fact that it moves me beyond any quick category of social comparison. No matter where I go, it seems as if I meet people who are only too ready to make me feel how poorly I fare on the social scale compared to them. How long can I go on being identified with brands of outer success that do not represent my inner self?

In connection with a retreat I gave in California to an audience of actors and executives in the film industry, I began to follow the career of one movie star who confessed to me that she had been chosen to do a picture not out of respect for her acting skills but for the in-demand popularity of her sex appeal. The public applause she got for her attractiveness overshadowed the sense of her value as a person. She played the studio game. She became a "sex symbol" so public relations teams could take her apart and then piece her together as an image for societal consumption. She looked at that publicity and knew it had little or nothing to do with the real woman she was. It wearied her to meet her fans and fair-weather friends on a make-believe basis.

As an actress, she had developed the art of repressing her true personality, of telling herself that she was happy being adored for what she was not. She made the effort to believe that she was this "sex symbol" only, but here at this retreat she began to sense the unhappiness in her heart. Underneath that glittering public image, she discovered a glaring emptiness, a paralyzed original life. Often she was unable to sleep at night because of her fear of this terrifying void. The utter loneliness of her real self—the self never met, never recognized, never loved for who she was—horrified her. In her worst moments she had contemplated the possibility of ending her life, but my conferences on original living had renewed her hope.

Though their lives were worlds apart, this movie star and my favorite cab driver were not much different. Both knew they were asking for unhappiness the moment they compared themselves with others. My wise friend saw with a smile that he was not a white-collar worker, a storekeeper, or anyone with a name. He did not base his contentment on the criteria of success held up by society. He tried to be mindful of his own originality, even to the point of admitting that he might have succeeded in any of these positions, but would he have been any happier than he was now? It occurred to me that the key to his joy was that he kept his eye on the incomparable inward dimension of his life. He thanked God that he had found his niche in society. That attitude of gratitude helped him to be a prince of a man for his passengers. He maintained his dignity and the sense of his original worth above and beyond any standards of comparison society might apply to him. He looked at others not with an envious eye that frantically measures and compares but with respect. He was not disgruntled because others seemed to do better than he. He was happy for them.

SELF-MOTIVATION AND PUBLIC OPINION

Anyone who respects his or her own originality bestows a respectful eye on the originality of others. To meet each person as unique is to rejoice in their accomplishments. We may only have gone as far as high school, but we admire their higher degrees and cultivated manner of speech. We are also aware that none of these traits reveals the unique humanity of a person. We greet the other, above and beyond these accomplishments, as the self they most deeply are. Because this approach is rather rare, others may either feel threatened or delighted by it. Much depends on where they stand in relation to their own originality at this moment of life.

The power of the standard by which we compare ourselves to one another cannot be discounted or taken lightly. In a phrase, it is public opinion. The public is everyone and no one in particular. It is everywhere and nowhere specifically. At times I am part of it. At other times I step aside, at least momentarily, from the impersonal one and become myself. The public watches television, listens to the radio, reads the newspaper, eyes the billboards along the highways, glances at advertisements in the bus or at window displays in department stores. The public is a generalization, a word for an ever-changing number of people in their anonymity.

What moves the public *as public* is not self-motivation, which is an extension of our originality and which makes us more than the mass. What the public craves is not this orientation to truth but whatever it is that keeps society on the move. A particular group, such as a family, club, or school, can be motivated to do public service and still respect each of its members, but the public as such tends to overlook the individual; it is not a specific group that subscribes to certain enduring principles and projects. It is that always changing, amorphous, anonymous mass that feels important and powerful because of its numbers. Public opinion is assumed to be exceedingly valuable as our fixation on polls reveals. Nobody knows precisely who holds these opinions, yet they have a hold on our appraisal powers. The public lauds these statistics and prompts us to act on basis of numbers only.

These fluctuating movements of public sentiment act like "reflexes" over which we have minimal control. There is nothing lasting about them.

What the public adores today, it may despise tomorrow. Public opinions are like fashions. Each one comes up as the "in" thing today only to be cast aside tomorrow by "the latest." Words like "new," "modern," "in," and "progressive" work like magic on the public. As soon as someone is able to convince the public that this person, event, or thing is "it," a reflex occurs and the amorphous body of the public begins to quiver with excitement. Everyone seems eager to mimic and move in that direction.

Another key word the public sphere cherishes is "success," which is a synonym for measurable accomplishment. If one can convince the public that some person, enterprise, or product is measurably successful, one has "it" made. A book becomes more popular simply because a celebrity pronounces it a best seller. Its content may be shallow and repetitious but at least it is readable, as easy to grasp as a "sound byte," and capable of satisfying the curiosity of the consumer. For the rest, it may be here today and gone tomorrow, but, after all, it is a best seller, be it a motivational handbook or a sex manual. The former purchase does not prove that the buyer is any more self-motivated than the latter proves that the reader is pornographically inclined. Both purchases exemplify the point that one who buys a publication *merely* because it is a best seller may well be a representative of the anonymous public, moved more by the reflexes that periodically pulsate through this body than by the search for truth.

Self-motivation within the public sphere is seldom appreciated. An original person might question the validity of what comes hot off the press. He or she would not make it the basis of every conversation, even at the risk of being dubbed by the public a "party pooper." Content as they are in their own interiority such originals may remind the public of its own, now lost, originality. Its resistance to being reminded of this fact often brings further dialogue to a halt.

The reflex life of the public relishes the anonymous phrase, "they said." One turns to the media to make sure one comes across as clever and important. To be "in" with the latest requires a minimum of self-reflection. Replacing it is the blind imitation of who's who is societal circles. Original persons are frequently forewarned not to inspire the masses to change by risking to stand alone. The thought of being away from the rest of the crowd makes "crowd-pleasers" anxious and afraid. Any sign of self-motivation may awaken them to their inner emptiness, arousing not admiration for original persons but envy of them. Their response is not to lift up each soul in his or her uniqueness but to level everyone to size until they come to know their place as mere numbers added to all the other statistics that equal the anonymous public.

Envy of originality is the seedbed of envious comparison. One forgets that the content of uniqueness can never be envied, for it represents gifts that no one else receives. Originality differs from the noticeable traits one may share in various degrees with many others like hair coloring and language skills. These can be compared. Uniqueness cannot. It follows that a society that lives by the dictates of comparison is bound to promote envy. In our age we are prone to envy those who do better on the scale of comparable talents than we ourselves accomplish. In brief, we tend to be envious of persons who manifest faithfulness to their own originality in an often unoriginal world.

ENVY OF ORIGINALITY

When I am envious, I look askance at what is of value in another person. I resent that it is not mine. One such value, lacking in many of us, is the courage to live in the light of our true self. The more faithful we are to who we are, the more envy we may evoke. How does the often hidden poison of envy of originality seep into our heart?

Two roommates, Pearl and Peggy, go to a dinner party. Both young women are well-mannered, nice-looking, and pleasant to talk with. While Pearl says all the right things, she somehow lacks spontaneity. Peggy makes similar remarks, yet shining through them, is the sparkle of her personality. Something fresh and attractive spills over when she expresses herself. It is difficult to trace the source of her charm. Pearl senses that her roommate has something she doesn't have. She tries to imitate Peggy's words and gestures. She succeeds at times, but the effect is not the same. Peggy's uniqueness eludes her. Pearl becomes aware of many instances in which Peggy's inner resources reveal themselves spontaneously.

Peggy brings this "difference factor" not only to a dinner party but to all she says and does. The simplest arrangement in her room bears the mark of her personhood. Pearl begins to feel, by contrast, the shallowness of her own life. She becomes irritated. Why does Peggy have what she doesn't? Peggy's poise and self-possession begin to bug her. Frustration with what she cannot be, becomes an obsession. With each passing day, the relaxed originality of the life of her roommate is harder to bear. She feels an angry wish to destroy what she herself cannot be, but she feels powerless to do so. The destructive drive she cannot unleash on Peggy turns back upon herself. She loathes herself because she cannot be more like the person Peggy is.

Growing vindictive, Pearl is always ready to put a damper on Peggy's joy. Each attempt to destroy her roommate's originality proves futile. It deepens the painful awareness of the impotence of her envy. She can spoil the incidental expressions of Peggy's personality, not her personality itself. Sometimes the feeling of spite runs so deep that were resentment a river she would drown in it. At other moments she would like to drop Peggy altogether, especially when her self-motivated life exasperates her beyond words. The envious mood motivating Pearl has so poisoned her life that she lives, as it were, a counter-life that needs the daily irritant of Peggy's presence to give her a sense of purpose. She cannot leave Peggy alone, but neither can she allow her to live her life unchecked and unhampered.

PATTERNS OF ENVY

Similar patterns may develop between colleagues, mothers and daughters, fathers and sons, teachers and students, employers and employees. Persons plagued by this kind of envy will pick up the faintest sign of selfhood in anyone who crosses their path. In a functional society it is easy to spot someone who is different. Anyone not yet assimilated as an anonymous member of the public stands out annoyingly.

Let us look again at the two women just described. Pearl is more intent on belittling Peggy's personality than on discovering and developing her own deepest self. She begrudges Peggy's self-reliance. She knows how demanding it would be to be herself, as Peggy is. To Pearl the best situation would be one in which neither she nor anyone else would be an original person. To her a group of girls in which no one would stand out is infinitely preferable to one that includes a number of girls who are themselves.

Envy of originality is malicious. Malice means that I slander the other or destroy what he or she has because of spite. A mother envious of a daughter who shows her own taste in fashion may use the barbed wire of malice to undermine her self-confidence. She may tell her daughter how ridiculous she looks: "Nobody will notice you, dear, in that kind of attire." In the meantime, mother may be aware that her daughter's taste is better than her own. She herself subscribes to trendy fashions simply because they represent "the latest." It is her daughter's originality in dress that she cannot bear. Envy prompts her sly insinuations of inadequacy, coated though they may be with the "honeytalk" of sweet concern.

NEARNESS AND THE INVIDIOUS EYE

A certain nearness to the envied person seems to favor the escalation of envy. Pearl, tormented by envy of Peggy's originality, would probably not be envious of the originality of the First Lady. Some of the First Lady's colleagues, however, may be devoured by the same envy Pearl shows toward Peggy. Nearness to the envied other may be on the rise due to growth in population; to the false belief that we are all equal in every respect; to the functional organization of schools, offices, and places of entertainment. We are rubbing shoulders constantly. Given such close quarters, we are more aware of the originality of others, more pained by it, and more demanding than ever that all be alike.

Envy of originality, may be more readily evoked because of the tight interdependency of society. In his daily life a rancher feels less plagued by envy over the originality of another rancher fifty miles away than a typist feels towards a person six feet from her whose personality she cannot miss.

The manifestations of uniqueness which evoke envy can be both simple and familiar. An extraordinary show of originality may not induce envy at all. Such originality seems to be so far out of reach that it may arouse little or no envy in the average person for whom looking at others with an invidious eye has not become a way of life.

Envy arises over simple manifestations of quiet self-motivation in a person relatively close to us. Pearl is upset by Peggy's spontaneous self-motivation because it is evident in the everyday ways of life in which both girls are equally engaged. If Peggy were to show surprising originality in some specialized field—if she were, for instance, a champion swimmer or a whiz in mathematics—Pearl would be less annoyed. However, to be a self-reliant, sparkling self in everyday life makes one think, "I could be just like her."

Perhaps the role nearness plays in envy can be traced to surroundings at home where an original child may have experienced the first hints of envy of originality. In childhood, this gift of uniqueness is only in its beginning stages. It cannot yet be realized in self-motivations true to one's interiority. The originality of childhood manifests itself mainly in spontaneity. Yet parents and children are already aware that one child may be more inclined to be him or herself than others. The child's originality is not yet a threat to the grown-ups around him. His spontaneous outbursts endear him to friends and relatives. He is so cute. Her antics evoke smiles of affectionate appreciation. However, brothers and sisters, who vie with the child for attention, feel that his or her spontaneity cuts into their share of it. They evoke in their siblings not appreciation but envy.

Later in life, envious children—now grown up—may vaguely fear that the family situation will repeat itself. They live in the expectation that somebody may steal the attention they want for themselves. Even if a person hides his originality, he will not necessarily succeed in avoiding envy. In a fairly homogenized group, let us say, of soldiers, office personnel, or factory workers, each one may unconsciously do his or her best to be as inconspicuous as possible. Nevertheless, envy can be evoked to a surprising degree when anyone unwittingly shows signs of uniqueness as a person. Others suddenly become aware of what they may lack. The person looked upon immediately senses their hostility. The family situation repeats itself. Because envy between younger children in the family is an almost universal symptom, it is unlikely that we can find a society in which the tendency to envy is totally absent.

DETESTATION OF ORIGINALITY

Two aspects of originality can especially evoke envy. Most visible is not the unique source of original living, which is rooted in the mystery at the center of one's life. What evokes envy first of all are the good effects blossoming forth from originality like joy and gratitude, good humor and humility, candor and courage. Only gradually may it dawn upon the onlooker that there is a connection between these virtues and the uniqueness that enabled them to emerge. The more I become envious of the fruits of originality, the more I envy and even detest the person in whom I see these and similar traits of character.

Envy of originality wells up from a secondary source when the envious person recognizes its absence in oneself. One then envies the original self one could have been. Soon self-envy spreads to the envy of all forms of unique self-motivation in society.

The reaction of children toward a child whose originality makes them feel deprived of similar gifts is to demand, so to speak, that the playing field be leveled. Anyone who is different threatens their share of attention. The inequality that is the normal result of originality seems intolerable to children. They can be merciless towards anyone who stands out from the crowd. Children do not yet recognize original dignity as the gift that it is. They know only that the child in question deprives them of attention. Children try to overcome or prevent the pain of envy by demanding the same treatment for all.

Grown-up children in a society of adults unconsciously repeat the leveling tactics of childhood. The real source of their demand for equality—envy of originality—goes unvoiced. Leveling is done in the name of solidarity, sociability, charity, orthodoxy. This envy—carried over from childhood into adult life—hinders the development of originality in society. It also hampers the healthy growth of the envious person him or herself.

A society that cannot profit from the unique self-motivations of its members is a crippled place. Our present day civilization imposes uniformity, among others, on its work force, which has become an extension of machines, computers, anonymous committees, and administrative schemes. This constant stress on uniformity often deteriorates into an implicit condemnation of any expression of spontaneity and self-motivation. In such a climate the leveling tendency of childhood, which a culture should help to overcome, is instead strengthened.

ENVY OF SELF—ENVY OF OTHERS

A university professor came to visit me for a confidential talk. "My problems are rather strange," he began. "I seem to be at war with myself." I hastened to assure him that this condition was a common one at some time or another.

"I know that," he said, "but my case seems different. I feel at war not so much with drives I cannot master but with what I cannot be. There is a war going on inside of me between who I am at present and who I could have been had my situation been different. I know that sounds strange to you but please let me try to explain what I mean.

"I am a happily married man. I have a wonderful wife and four fine children. My academic career is moderately successful, but believe it or not, I am plagued by the idea of how much farther I might have advanced had I not been married. Family life takes a lot of energy and attention that takes away the time I used to have for research and study. Before I married, I published a lot. I was slowly making a name for myself. I was invited to speak at other colleges. All of this notoriety has tapered off since my marriage. At first it did not bother me, but lately I have become obsessed by that other fellow in me, that famed scholar, I could have been were it not for my family.

"I began to tell myself that this kind of thinking is nonsense. I was an average but well-liked teacher—no great shakes as a scholar on the national level, but respected by my colleagues and above all a man loved and esteemed by my wife and children. Still that other fellow in me— that self that I could have been—kept gnawing at me.

"I imagined that there he was, free from family care, with ample time to read, write, and travel, with enough money for books, equipment, and scientific trips. He was well groomed and rested when he appeared before an appreciative public. I became envious of that other person that I was on the road to becoming before I got married. In reaction, I began to malign his scholarship, to hate his success. I started to find fault with his imagined appearances at various schools throughout the country; I depreciated his trips abroad, his fancy interests in high level conferences.

"Soon my predicament grew worse. I had belittled him so well that I began to believe the scenarios I had conjured up. It became a tough task for me to be content with a normal day in my office. It got so bad that class preparation became a bore. It was almost impossible to write an article for a professional journal. I began to neglect my appearance. In my envious detraction of that other person in me, I came to depreciate those dimensions of life in which he was and still could be a success.

"I was in a dilemma. If I admitted to myself that my academic work was valuable, I felt overcome by envy for the prominent professor I dreamt of being had I pursued a full-time career instead of getting married. If I did not value my academic work, I might no longer feel envy for that other "me" of whom I could say: "After all, his was a rather insignificant occupation with not much to show for it." The more I believed that lie, the less I was able to give myself wholeheartedly to my teaching tasks and occasional accomplishments.

"What is worse, I came not only to devalue my own scholarly life; I began to make light of the academic zeal of others. I felt annoyed when anyone made a fuss over a person's achievement as a scholar or speaker. I discovered to my surprise that I had become as envious of the person who was praised as I was of that other self in me that I could have been."

EYING MYSELF WITH ENVY

Strange as it may seem, I can be envious of myself. I can cast a spiteful eye on some dimension of my personality. I may then experience a split between the "me" who is envious of others and the "me" envied by myself. This division is possible because of two domains that threaten to erode the truth of my originality. One has to do with the limits set by my always situated freedom. I simply cannot be all things to all people all of the time! The other has to do with the fantasy life I imagine would make me happy but which for any number of reasons I cannot attain. Such visions of grandeur only exist in my imagination; they cannot be harmonized with the demands of daily life. Nonetheless such potential selves, unsituated and imagined, may clamor for recognition. They may even develop in isolation from the otherwise harmonious unfolding of my life as a whole.

Such an "as if" mode of existence focused on what could have been may be composed of a tightly interwoven set of wish fulfillments and unrealistic desires. At moments I may become aware of these strange forces churning inside me like an otherwise quiet stream after a storm. They point to values I long to attain but cannot realistically actualize in my life here and now. Compared with the boredom of my daily routine these unfulfilled ambitions seem to beckon me to a far more exciting way of life than that which is concretely mine. Such imagined potentials are lived for the most part in a dream world disconnected from reality. They are not limited by the resistance that hinders the realization of these idle fantasies in daily life. How exciting such as yet unrealized modes of living seem to be in comparison to the steady growth demanded of me in my everyday surroundings!

No wonder that the real me may be inclined to look spitefully at these exciting underdeveloped lives within me. I feel envious of their beckoning horizons, the more so when I see signs that others have reached what I can never attain. Instead of thanking God for my gifts, I envy theirs. I do not accord them the respect I should have for any value attained by me or others. Envy replaces respect the moment I fail to admit that there is no situation on earth where we can live all our longings to the full.

Self-envy is due to an absence of relaxed self-respect for my limits and blessings. It may lead to repression or denial of parts of me that remain true even if they are not yet nor, for that matter, can ever be realized. My willful blindness to the richness of the ordinary causes these tensions to proliferate. My inner life becomes loaded with unsettled feelings and unfilled desires that may erupt with volcanic force into my thoughts, words, and actions. I experience an outbreak of envious inclinations I cannot explain, many of which seem at odds with the person I know I am called to be.

EYING OTHERS WITH ENVY

Interwoven with self-envy is envy of others. I may meet another person who lives in a way I admire but know I cannot emulate. Against my better judgment, I may begin to look at them with as much envy as I looked on myself. In sly ways, unnoticed in polite society, I mock their life style and demean their profession. I see the fault-lines in the values they radiate without even knowing it. I feel uneasy when I hear others praise them. Do they not see how vainglorious their so-called selfless actions really are?

Were I aware of the depths of my own self-envy, I might be able to discern the source of my irritation. Self-envy mobilizes my energy to deny and devalue the ordinary life I ought to have lived. This distorted perspective then evokes tension between the real me and the envied me. Every time someone looks appreciatively at similar values in another's life, I feel ill at ease. My hitherto successful repression of them threatens to break through. Praise of that forgotten value invites me to view it with appreciation, but I cannot. Frantically, I mobilize more energy to fight the threat of self-disclosure. I feel alarmed because others seem to resurrect desires I thought were buried. The attractiveness of their life endangers the defenses that have enabled me to dismiss the pathways of original living I have repressed wittingly or unwittingly. The result is that I tend to depreciate the freer responses I see alive in others.

The sting of envy doubles in intensity when friends and strangers alike express admiration for the persons I devalue. The slightest sign of recognition threatens to awaken the truth that I have not only devalued them but also undervalued my own gifts. These unfulfilled parts of my life lead to further resentment of anyone who seems happier than I. No matter what I accomplish, it never seems good enough. A depressive dissatisfaction invades my being like a fog that will not lift. Instead of being myself, I am tortured by the desire to be more like the envied other, yet it is their reputation I want secretly to destroy. On some level of awareness, I can taste the poison of envy, but its power has already seeped into the very fabric of my life. It feels as if the only way to be saved from this calamity is to respond to each increase of public praise for this person with subtle reminders of his or her faults. I become a master in devaluation, arousing suspicion where none is deserved and convincing myself that I am the only one who can keep the envied other humble and no different from anyone else.

I soon feel compelled to find cohorts with whom to share my concern. Envy causes me to focus on real or imagined flaws that escape others' attention. I become a master in conveying the latest tidbit of gossip about them that comes my way. I point to the possible threat the envied person may pose to their interests. Envy like a virus is contagious. It corrodes the ability to respect others and compels me instead to distort their gifts every chance I get.

DESTRUCTIVE POWER OF ENVY

Visiting friends, George meets an unexpected guest. He strikes him as a charming man, poised and engaging. At first George likes Justin. Then other feelings come to the fore. His charm makes George aware of his awkwardness. He feels clumsy in his presence and out of place. It is difficult for George to admit that Justin has gifts he does not. Why does he attract everyone's attention? His manners irk George more and more. Can't others see through that smooth facade of his? George says to himself: "I know his kind. He seems to sense that I don't like him." George becomes self-conscious. His words flow less easily. The atmosphere in the room becomes strained. Soon he feels like the spoiler of the evening. Nobody echoes his envious attitude. He seems to be the loser. It becomes impossible for him to appreciate the good in this new acquaintance or to learn anything from him. Worse than this, George cuts himself off from his own potential for graciousness.

How different the evening could have been had George been able to admire Justin or at least to find something pleasing in him. He might have spoken less sharply than he did. He could have uncovered his own possibility for gentility, sustained the mood of pleasant company, and helped to create an agreeable atmosphere. Life for all of the guests that evening would have been less edgy and more elegant. Now George eases toward the door, loath to admit that his envy has all but destroyed the evening.

CONFLICT OF ATTITUDES

The rendition of this experience enables us to note the difference between an attitude that is envious and one that is respectful. Envy is a mode of isolation: it closes us off from others. Respect is a mode of appreciation: it puts us in tune with the potency for goodness in all people; at the same time it opens us to new avenues of creativity in ourselves.

The difference between these two attitudes can be seen in the way we look at others. When my look is envious, I do not really see them. Inwardly I begin to belittle them. Outwardly I mock their manners or parody their behavior. Because I never really see them, nothing they do can be good in my eyes. My first look is one of envy.

It is interesting to note that the word "envy" comes from the Latin verb *invidere*, which means "to look askance at," "to look maliciously or spitefully into," "to cast an evil eye upon," "to envy or begrudge something." Is this not exactly what George did? He looked askance at Justin's gentlemanly behavior. He cast, as it were, an evil eye upon his etiquette. Primitive people believed that the evil eye could spoil, sicken, or kill the other. The envious eye is not that different. It implies a spiteful look loaded with destructive feelings.

Once I look upon the other as an object of envy, I am unable to rejoice in their originality or to emulate any part of it. Instead I proceed in the opposite direction--trying to deny this value in them and in myself. Envy impoverishes the mutuality in our world of meaning and becomes the source of faulty perception, judgment, and action. Envying the engaging manners of a guest offers a good example. If I allow envy to escalate, I may come to reject sincere graciousness as phony in every situation. To maintain my envious perspective, I am obliged to belittle expressions of gentility in other people and to fight off an appreciative awareness of this virtue in myself. Were I to value my own graciousness, I could not deny the worth of the same gift in others. Like a slow moving sickness, envy spreads through the fabric of life as a whole.

Respect offers the opposite outlook. This word comes from the Latin verb *respicere*, which means "to look again," "to look benevolently," "to give the other the good eye," "to cast a favorable eye upon." Like envy, respect is an attitude toward people in whom certain values shine forth. Had George been able to look at Justin with respect, he might have seen many values to admire. He could have looked not at but upon this new acquaintance with appreciative attention.

A respectful look nourishes our humanity and deepens our spirituality. Had he been able to confirm Justin's gracious demeanor instead of condemning it, George could have grown in sensitivity for any manifestation of gentility that came his way. By the same token, he could have been more sensitive to his own possibility to grow in graciousness. Respectful seeing facilitates the realization of the admired virtue I see in others. Envious seeing, on the contrary, erodes any manifestation of this value, causing spite to increase and admiration to decrease.

ENVY AND RESPECT

Respect and envy spawn two different worlds of meaning, one attitude being humanizing, the other dehumanizing. Respect leads to a self-forgetful participation in what is of value wherever it reveals itself. Such a disposition is difficult to maintain in a society dominated by an inordinate striving for fame and fortune. In such a climate, I may experience the value of others as a threat to my own status or position. I fear that they may harm my career, diminish my popularity, or cast a shadow on my reputation, simply by outshining me.

The envious look separates us from one another. It isolates us in small worlds of our own making to be protected at any price. Envy closes us off from each other and from the mystery of love that nourishes our humanity. Respect hastens our redemption from isolation whereas envy only deepens our despair. Respect strengthens the common bonds that hold humanity together. It opens us to the light of truth and dispels the distorting perceptions on which the "green monster" of envy thrives.

SAFEGUARDING ORIGINALITY IN SOCIETY

Certain insights help us to safeguard original living in the midst of a society envious of originality and prone to turn us into hyper-functional servants of our schedules. The secret aim of a mechanistic civilization may be to engulf us in public opinion polls and a slew of leveling customs that determine every move we make. Population growth around the world warrants a rigorous organization of production and services. Professionals in many fields have no choice but to devise means of consumption, employment, education and health care. Our choice is not between collective structures or no structures at all but between blind conformity or reasonable creativity. Do we allow ourselves to be absorbed to such a degree by an organizational mentality and its insistence on efficiency and measurable outcomes that we forfeit any semblance of self-motivation and originality? We cannot survive without societal supports but neither can we thrive as human beings without taking a critical stance toward the tendency to reduce respect for uniqueness to an impersonal consent to the demands devised by collective organizations. Modern society has become a web of functional structures in which each of us is caught to some degree. They tend to be more collectivistic than communal, more media-propelled than personally responsible for the equality in dignity that is our birthright.

People used to live in towns or villages where it was possible to know one another in neighborhood groups, to share a common faith, and to work side by side for a good purpose. Finding places like this in present-day society is like unearthing a rare treasure. Pluralistic populations are not bound together by a unity of beliefs. We do not know, as tribesmen or medieval villagers did, the story behind the life of each individual we meet. We have become strangers to one another, packed together in large metropolitan centers where we hardly know the family next door. We are there neither by choice nor preference but by economic necessity.

Social and monetary pressures fling us together in unwieldy movements and associations increasingly difficult to oversee. The need for education herds children into enormous school systems with countless others who may share nothing more than age, citizenship, and the imposition of compulsory education.

Many of us do not know each other as unique persons but as purveyors of services with various professional, utilitarian, technical, or educational skills. We are encouraged to outdo one another on the social and business scale. We do not share a story based on affective togetherness beginning in early childhood and lasting throughout life. Instead we are staff members of large corporations geared to mass production. We labor monotonously to succeed, cut off from the visible effects of our work. We may have no immediate experience of making an impact on society despite all that we do.

Surfacing these concerns may be a first step in countering many of the collectivistic conditions that promote the leveling process. Now is the time to recommit ourselves to the goal of preserving and fostering our originality by resisting the often silent but deadly process of envious disrespect. Not only does it harm others; it also robs us of our own self-motivation. We resent the fact that others may be trying to regain in their life what we have lost, betrayed, or never discovered in ours. They may remind us of the truth we would like to forget--that of our unique-communal life call before God. In a leveling society this reminder may be so threatening it must be crushed. Yet in the end we have no choice but to respect our gifts and use them for the good of all without a hint of envy.

Chapter Two
Tactics of Envy

The tactics of envy may or may not be familiar to us. As much as we might hope never to meet up with them, we probably will. What matters is that we refuse on principle to become enlisted in the devious campaigns in which they tempt us to participate. We may lessen the chances of our being duped by these envious feelings and their subtle workings by a study of them.

Unfortunately the relatively tame incidents of envy in ordinary life may not tell us much about the depths of destruction into which envy of originality may sink. Everyday situations may be so veiled by politeness that we fail to notice the subtle poison released by the sly tactics of envy. To see them clearly, we must enlarge them beyond normal size. By means of such magnification, we may begin to suspect what may happen to us on a smaller scale if and when we experience envy ourselves or convey it to others. We may also see the damage caused whenever we forfeit respect for the gift of our uniqueness.

To observe envious tactics at work, we need to consider cases in which envy of originality has become a way of life, indeed an obsession. Such malice may occur for various reasons. A pretentious functionary, a lazy or mediocre person, a fanatical conformist—these and other types may become the purveyors of obsessive envy. They sense the threat originality poses to their "killjoy" mentality. Though such cases may be exceptional, we can see them in the same way as we look into distorting mirrors that expose the irregular features of our face. We may deny that we look like that, but we still begin to notice traits we did not suspect we had before we were exposed to these exaggerations.

Our study has to include obsessively envious persons as well as obviously original ones. The latter evoke envy even when their originality may not be that noticeable. Still the sincerity of their self-motivation in service of God and others evokes envious looks. The quality of their communication and the efficacy of their actions make them vulnerable to invidious comparisons.

Obviously original persons often express their originality in humble, not striking, achievements. They may be more original privately than they are known to be publicly, but they are no less likely to draw the ire of obsessively envious persons. For this reason, the best way to observe the tactics of envy is to see what happens when a truly original person collides with someone obsessed by envy.

OBSESSIVE ENVY AND OBVIOUS ORIGINALITY

What happens when envy of originality becomes an obsession? Consider the predicament of a "bottom line" salesman who has adapted himself to this policy and donned the appearance of a courteous person with a fixed smile on his face. He meets his obligations by perfecting his apparent form at the price of depreciating his own uniqueness. He suppresses as often as possible how he feels and does whatever is necessary to make a sale. He adopts the rules of success others write without making them his own. He does not question their meaning nor does he dare to suggest another approach to customer satisfaction. He knows that the opinion he risks offering today can get him into trouble tomorrow when another idea emerges as more current or correct.

Yet he wants to feel worthwhile; he likes it when his performance evokes a customer's praise. He works hard at any enterprise he can accomplish within his self-imposed frame of being better safe than sorry. As long as he blocks any awakening of his repressed selfhood, he feels fine. Surrounded by people caught in the same grip of envy, he gains the applause he needs to sustain his achievements. Getting a leg up on the other salesmen in the company improves his position. He determines to learn every detail of the operation so he can translate it into higher sales. A stickler for detail, he shows up at every meeting and only contributes ideas that make him look more clever than his peers. The monotonous mood of this depersonalized life fits him to a "T."

At home he adopts the posture of a model parent, solicitous of his spouse but adept at avoiding serious conversations with her or the children. As long as nobody makes waves, everybody will be happy. If an original insight intrudes into his rituals of professionalism or parenthood, he dismisses it as a threat to his established routines. Conformity to the impersonal "they" is the best formula for success. He feels slight waves of envy toward those who do as well or better than he in functional performance so he forces himself to behave better than they could while compelling himself not to advance beyond them in ingenuity and inventiveness.

Everything goes smoothly until his "don't rock the boat" formula for living is upset by the appearance of a unique person. He pretends to feel at ease with him when he breaks the code of polite conversation and lets his personal feelings be known in administrative meetings, but he lacks the cleverness to manipulate committee decisions; he does not know how to walk away from painful deliberations smelling like a rose; he has less data at his fingertips. Envy of his colleague compels him to say to himself, "I feel sorry for him. The idea that I could envy such a bumbling operator is preposterous."

Then the unexpected happens. Some of the ideas of the envied other begin to catch on. The boss likes them. In committee meetings, the board swings toward his proposals. Their approval of this upstart makes him feel uneasy: "After all, my know-how outshines his originality." To beat him to the punch, he tries to come up with some ideas of his own, but to his consternation, he has great difficulty proposing anything new, let alone daring. Repression of originality in the personal sphere seems to have affected his inventiveness on the functional level.

The situation worsens when he invites this competitor to visit him at his home. His wife and children respond warmly to such a personable guest. He goes to great lengths to steer their attention to his idiosyncrasies. Then he changes tactics and joins in their praise. At the same time, he jokes about his bumptious character and lack of finesse, but to his dismay, they assure him these traits are endearing! They are intrigued by the way in which his colleague engages others. This is too much for him to take! He begins to suspect that in spite of his sly put-downs of this new employee, he may manifest a quality or two he misses. That's when the envious eye begins to blink with renewed fury.

By the end of the evening, after the last good-bye, he pours himself a night-cap and forces himself not to think about that long ago time when he was less manipulative and more open to learn. It is too threatening to contemplate the past. Similar feelings return the minute he lets down his guard. He denounces and devalues his own original self. Instead he concludes that peers and company managers were wrong to be taken in by this phony. Envy lets him spy like a hawk flaws in his so-called creative contributions. In the field of salesmanship they *must* be unsubstantiated; in the arena of administration, they *must* be at odds with the facts; in the context of religion, they *must* be heretical.

At first cautiously, then more boldly, he starts to express his suspicions: "There's something about that colleague of ours I'm not sure we can trust. In the end people like him tend to be somewhat unbalanced. We should exercise caution before giving him our approval." By expressing his envy modestly, he conceals its intensity. Vehement feelings are frowned upon in polite society, so he projects the image of a wise, sober, realistic person. Talking excitedly might turn the suspicions he has evoked on him. Others might jump to the conclusion that he is prejudiced. He wants them to feel that he is moved by common sense, by concern for the company and its customers. He can discredit the envied other more effectively when he shows temperance.

His next pronouncement ups the stakes: "Personally I have nothing against him. It's refreshing to hear new ideas. Of course, he tends to call too much attention to himself. He probably doesn't realize how bad he makes the rest of us look." Having established himself in the minds of other gossipers as the voice of reason, he escalates his attack: "I like him, but, let's face it, there is *something* about him that is not quite right." First he presents himself as a man of prudence and kind but critical discernment. His cohorts are "regular guys," who appreciate moderation. Then he allows feelings of suspicion to creep into the conversation. They catch on like a smoldering match to the tinder of depreciation and the firestorm starts. He suggests discreetly that this gentleman is not whom he seems. Nobody knows what makes him tick. This sobering suggestion is enough to evoke a vague uneasiness about him in several other employees who, like him, have made the leveling of self-motivated persons their mission in life. They sense the excitement envy evokes once the trap is set. Soon they come to him, confidentially sharing their concern about the danger this well-meaning person presents to the company and the community it serves. They realize, of course, that most people in their goodness and simplicity do not suspect the threat he represents, but they knew from the beginning that he, a man with years of experience, would see through this upstart and be able to bring to light the faults they had already begun to suspect.

Now the campaign to rid the company of this original person gains steam. Even people in higher administration echo his critique. It feels good to be on the side of the seers. It restores his self-respect to be supported by like-minded fellows. He assures himself that he has an obligation to temper the rash enthusiasm displayed by those who hired him, to say nothing of his family who enjoyed his visit. He confesses that he, too, was taken in for a while by such a charming fellow, but now his better judgment has been confirmed by his superiors. He discovers to his delight that many of those who at first admired him feel uneasy about him. They are relieved to find a repertoire of reasons to cut him down to size.

Before long, quite a few people spend their time around the coffee bar enlightening others about the dangers this person poses. The instigator begins to work on some of his influential friends. They tell him it is up to them to protect all echelons of the company against the threat this stranger poses. Envy excels in enlisting others in their cause. They are eager to be identified with those who want to maintain the status quo. As the virus of envy spreads, the number of those infected by it increases. At the right moment, it might be possible to turn them into a symbolic lynching mob. This pretentious climber faces the painful possibility, innocent though he may be, of the gradual destruction of his reputation and career.

ESCALATING TACTICS OF ENVIOUS PERSONS

Persons obsessed by envy usually operate behind the scenes. They undermine others who are self-motivated, not by legal means or public discussion but by insinuation, ridicule, and the arousal of suspicion. Their accusations would fail within the framework of jurisprudence or open debate, so they turn instead to camouflage. They go around the codes and structures of society in an attempt to corrupt the reputation of the envied other. When he or she makes a perfectly human mistake, envious persons are on the alert to draw attention to this fact. They develop, so to speak, a "sixth sense" for spotting any fault, even to the point of trying to trick someone into making a mistake. They are delighted when they get the victim of envy to say something in excitement that can later be used against him or her. They take what was said out of context and display this gossipy gem at meetings or social gatherings. They quote the incident persistently, savoring each word that might make the original person look bad in the eyes of others. Every time they distort the story a little more, though they are clever enough to disguise their damaging information as good-natured, anecdotal banter so as not to endanger their own reputation. Their story gladdens and amuses their listeners, many of whom have no lost love for people who choose to be themselves.

The fact that an original person is not like other people arouses the indignation of envious types. What they disapprove of is one's uniqueness, originality, and self-motivation. They frown upon these traits not only in him or her but in all people, including themselves!

Envious dispositions express themselves in habits of leveling all that is unique about a person's life. What envy despises is not one's pursuit of excellence but one's uniqueness. Their true self is the target. One's undaunted selfhood—the source of his or her creative ingenuity and fresh perceptions—that is the target envious types will go to any length to destroy. If possible, they will resort to slander, censorship, "burning at the stake," or other forms of symbolic or real killing.

The goal of a life dominated by envy is the death of the original person. To be sure, envious persons do not demand this destruction openly. They do not even know that they want it to happen. Their wish for a creative person's demise is expressed symbolically in their attempt to destroy his or her reputation or the way one evokes genuine admiration in the minds and hearts of others. They become masters at spotting any vulnerability in another's character. Their aim is to break down the respect they find in friends or strangers for a self-motivated person.

Symbolic sacrifice of unique people is justified by the rationalization that it serves the common good. It is better for one person to die than for all the people to perish. Symbolic murders like these are perpetrated in good conscience. The passionately anti-original person feels that it is his or her duty in life to do away with innovators and creative thinkers. Gossip and slander become their main weapons. They find in them a way of escaping awareness of their own murderous wishes while still giving in to them. They imagine themselves to be charismatic figures, delegated by fate to safeguard the common good.

The scene of symbolic assassination may assume ritualistic proportions, not unlike human sacrifice in certain cultures. It was often the most outstanding person who was designated to die as an offering to the gods. Envy may have influenced the selection. The tribe could admit the assets of its victims and, at the same time, eliminate them without embarrassment. Should not only the best among them be offered to the gods? By destroying an outstanding person ritually, the tribe escaped the self-torture of envy. The immolation enabled them to preserve their capacity for admiration. They did not have to deny the value of their victims. On the contrary, their gifts made them more worthy as sacrifices. In some cases the tribe carried its envy over to the gods. The gods were envious of gifted people. To placate them they had to be slain ritually.

Religious justifications for the assassination of prominent people are not alien to contemporary society. Beneath the veneer of modern consciousness primitive urges lurk like a slow acting poison. Envious persons in our era may justify their symbolic immolation of original people with arguments reminiscent of a tribal past. They may carry their own envy to symbolic proportions, coating the sacrificial process with religious significance. They may go so far as to conclude that their god suffers from the originality shown by self-motivated people, who are really full of pride and conceit. The god of justice whom they serve looks with a spiteful eye on original persons. They are a cause of scandal and a temptation to others. As well-balanced, unassuming conformists, who have the best interests of others at heart, they feel obliged in their unworthiness to be the humble inquisitors, the holy hangmen of these annoying originals.

At times slanderous words and gestures take on an almost ritualistic aura, expressed with unctuous conviction. One's voice sinks to a confidential whisper. One's face features shocked indignation about the outrageous words and actions of these self-motivated souls. Listeners are quickly drawn into an atmosphere of righteous indignation. They feel holy outrage that such types dare to offend the gods by the hubris of their creativity. Their voices become hushed; their tone conspiratorial. Together they immolate the envied other symbolically, out of love and for the public good. Meanwhile, they reassure each other that this sacrifice is necessary. They repeat in a variety of ways that it is their duty to silence these upstarts for the good of the whole community. At the end of such a ceremony, they may feel the satisfaction that comes after a duty well done, a ritual performed to perfection.

Their victims, in the meantime, may involve themselves in an engrossing enterprise in service of others. Intensely occupied as they are, they mind their own business. They pay no attention to the tactics of envious schemers. Strategically, they should spend more time at social gatherings and committee meetings, in cafeterias and cocktail hours. Perhaps they could then undo the evil image of themselves that these detractors have built up.

However, to fight scheming with more scheming would only destroy them as the persons they are. Trying to meet their opponents on their ground would endanger their own integrity. Their major concern would switch from dedication to the task before them to energy-depleting assessment of what other people whisper about them. All they would gain by trying to address these rumors would be a loss of time and a depletion of their inner equanimity. Their attention would run in wild patterns since there is no rhyme or reason to gossip. Eroded would be their own capacity for respect and admiration. Were that to happen, then envious persons would win in an ultimate sense: they would have perverted the respectful person by infecting him or her with their poison.

Neither would it do much good to victims of envy to give up a successful enterprise to placate the ire of those around them. They may harbor the illusion that the spiteful objections directed at them are evoked by some pernicious features of their current pursuits of which they are unaware. In truth, envy of originality is not aroused by this or that engagement. The uniqueness of the person him or herself is the object of the invidious stare. To satisfy their detractors, creative people may shift to a modest, less controversial undertaking, but that, too, evokes criticism. Experience tells them that changing from project to project does not work. They realize that the only way to please their opponents would be for them to vanish from the face of the earth. Nothing may have been wrong with their work. They themselves were the problem. Their unique approach to their profession aroused in those around them the one result they could not tolerate. The unforgivable sin in a leveling society is simply to be oneself.

Another group of people ripe for the arousal of envy consists of those who make it a habit to impersonate men and women of importance. Being neither passionately committed to a good cause nor personally resourceful themselves, they cherish few opinions or feelings of their own. They do not scorn self-motivated people, but neither do they respect them. They might not be inclined to harm them but neither would they say a word to protect their reputation or position. Since it seems important to appear a cut above others, they are prone to name-dropping and repeating the utterances of persons who seem to carry more weight in society than they do.

The few for whom the destruction of originality has become a way of life may succeed in tricking them into watching every move made by annoying upstarts. Ambitious imitators are eager to parrot important insider information. They do not mean to ruin self-motivated victims by such gossip. They seek only confirmation of their assessments by those who seem to be "in" at the moment. In short, they swing in whatever direction the wind of envy blows. They pick up the chant that this show-off is out for him or herself. They feel obliged to protect their circle against impending dangers. They mimic the excitement with which ponderous pronouncements against their victims are uttered. This pretense of shocked indignation makes them feel ripe and ready for a change. Because this feeling is so seductive, they are on the prowl to be enlisted in any leveling project.

Envious instigators may succeed in turning people of influence and their imitators against the originals around them. Dormant in the population at large is a latent envy of all those whose success makes them feel less privileged. Without their cooperation, agitators against self-motivated persons would not be able to reach the point of their real or symbolic demise. Usually one does not have a chance to attack outstanding persons so when such an opportunity presents itself, the crowd rallies around it. The moment self-motivated persons begin to lose their name and position, one can sense the thinly disguised glee of envious people, who sit in smug judgment knowing they got what they deserved.

IRRITATION EVOKED BY ANYONE WHO IS OBVIOUSLY ORIGINAL

Original persons remind others plagued by envy of the life that could have been theirs had they not crippled their potential for creative living. Facing self-motivated people makes impersonal ones feel exposed. The originality they witness threatens their anonymity. For an anxious moment, they feel isolated from the source of their self-justification, namely, the anonymous public. They hate to be reminded of the inequality between people in the realm of originality, talent, and possibility. They like to believe, in principle if not in fact, that they could have been cast into similar administrative, professional, and social roles had they been given the same chance. They prefer the illusion that there are only interchangeable roles: anyone can assume them when a vacancy arises, provided he or she is in the right place at the right time.

The "envy of position" differs from the "envy of selfhood," which may be loosened the moment an original person so much as appears on the scene. He or she deviates from the unwritten rule that nobody is irreplaceable. Many people envision the model society as a flawless machine wherein each homogenized part should be replaceable by another. All that matters is that the person concerned have the proper training. In their minds one serves the collectivity best by homogenizing oneself so completely that one is always available to replace any missing "piece of equipment," with no consideration for his or her own motivation, talent, and temperament.

While this omni-availability is impossible, it may be exalted as an ideal plan. All that is required of us is that we forfeit our potential for a personal life. Self-motivation is an annoying obstacle to the realization of this aim. Any time we remind others of their repressed desire to be themselves, our presence may be perceived as irritating. Keeping this desire under wraps has succeeded so far. The sheer presence of the envied other now threatens to rock the boat, evoking in the process embarrassment, guilt, shame, and anger. Were the message of originality permitted free rein, the dormant volcano on which a leveling society is built might suddenly erupt.

SOCIAL POSITION OF SELF-MOTIVATED PEOPLE

The social position of self-motivated people is another target for envy since it may threaten the chances of their secretly envious co-workers for promotion. Their position may be especially in jeopardy when someone poisoned by envy becomes their superior. Bosses like this feel supported in their leveling tactics by the latent envy of other staff members and employees. They sense that they can make almost any move against the envied other and probably be applauded in their efforts by most of the employees.

The boss in question may have climbed the ladder of success by slavish compliance with people who have already made it. Servility to the system put him on top of the person he secretly envied and feared. Now this man or woman depends on him for their means of subsistence. He awaits their anxious attempts to please him. He watches the awkward way in which they try to hide their ideas and feelings—not out of personal weakness but out of concern for their livelihood.

This behavior elates the boss. The anxiety he evokes in self-motivated persons gives him a sense of power. Their fate rests in his hands. Caution and flattery will not cure the envy of the boss. One should never expect to win the battle for acceptance. One may pretend that he is a team player, not worthy of the least bit of envy, but to no avail. No matter how one tries to hide it, it is clear that he or she is still their own person. It is only the weakness of their social position that reduces them to such displays of subjugation.

To respect his subordinates in their selfhood would imply a revolution on the part of the boss. He would have to open his eyes not only to the uniqueness of this employee but to his own selfhood as well. This awareness could invite a change in his attitudes and actions. At the same time, it would imply a willingness on his part to risk arousing the envy of the leveling community of workers that have become his support system.

ENVIOUS OR RESPECTFUL LOOKS

A life of leveling envy thrives in a climate of suspicion and condemnation. Envy excludes the appreciative look of respect. Envy's refusal to "look again" makes the condemnation of original persons inflexible and absolute. Respectful people, by contrast, experience their views as tentative. Their minds are open to new perspectives. Valuable sides of another's personality may cast doubt on their former opinion. They decide to look again because they can never see all at once who someone really is. New insights light up for them, making them wait a while before they pass judgment.

The envious look cast by closed types is one of certitude. They pride themselves on the unshakeability of their opinions. They seek to have them confirmed by "facts" and "common sense." They do not look twice at the persons they chide. What they look for are words and incidents that justify their disapproval. They dislike people who are moved by their original call because they are unpredictable. They threaten the familiar scheme of things.

Under the cover of their ponderous self-assurance, like a virgin spring waiting to be tapped, may be the hidden source of their own spontaneity. They dare not risk uncovering it since its disclosure could invite them to pursue a new style of life. To follow the call of their true self is an adventure they may not be ready or willing to pursue. Instead they may succumb to the illusion envy promotes that they are the privileged ones who can figure others out once and for all.

WILLFUL MEDIOCRITY AND ANTI-ORIGINALITY

Impersonal enviers may assess their own talents and gifts as modest but reasonable. They take pride in being reliable workers, who obey orders and seldom, if ever, step out of line. They don't find the risk of expressing what they feel really worth it. They are nice people who are in no way different from the others around them. By no means do they feel embarrassed by the drabness of their life. They are proud of it. They declare, perhaps a bit too strongly, that they are delighted to be that way. Notwithstanding how impersonal their life already is, they take every precaution to make it more so. They stick close to those like themselves, who are motivated more by public opinion than by personal integrity. They prefer to live in compliance with successful types exactly like themselves. They embrace with relief their style of life and its lack of self-motivation. In their envious attempts to level original people, they exalt conformity as an end in itself. For them, impersonal performance within academic, economic, or political organizations is the best safeguard against any expression of heartfelt concern. As far as they can tell, their public sense and practical know-how absolve them from any obligation to think about life in an original way. The surest road to success is that paved by mediocrity and anti-originality.

COMMON SENSE DISTINGUISHED
FROM COMMON WISDOM

When in everyday life we say, "He or she has common sense," it usually means that one is a relatively prudent and thoughtful person. This well deserved accolade may take on a different meaning for a mediocre functionary, fearful of personal reflection. "Public sense" might be a more accurate expression. This kind of sense must be distinguished from "common wisdom." The latter gift may be attributed to simple people, who may never be inventive in an unusual way but who have not betrayed

43

their personhood and who have the courage to remain faithful to their own modest self. They are wise enough to recognize that their life should be enlightened by the wisdom of humanity and the respect one ought to have for the truth others have been gifted to disclose. Because respect permeates their life, they are creative, not in the sense of inventing something new but in terms of a penetration into the mystery hidden in the words, acts, and customs of admirable souls.

Such common wisdom opens them to hidden values embedded in the traditions of generations. They do not copy them exactly, but they do try to live them uniquely. In this sense openness to value-radiation makes them creative. A learned person who would choose to remain mediocre as a human being is less wise than a simple man or woman whose self-motivation shows itself in his or her respectful demeanor. Though one's capacity for thought, speech, and action may be limited, though one does not easily catch the attention of others, at an unexpected moment one's hidden nobility may come to the fore. In contrast to their courage, envious types, who have chosen to forfeit their originality and remain mediocre, may abandon ship when the times get tough. Long after valueless people have fled, simple people may stay the course and perform heroic deeds.

ATTITUDES AND ACTIONS PERMEATED BY ENVY

Envy of selfhood cannot be confined to one dimension of the envied person; it spills over into other dispositions and actions. Affability may be tainted by an all-pervading envy of what is unique. Kindly acceptance of another may cover up the unvoiced apprehension that in no way must one reveal oneself as the person one is with one's own unique-communal life call. Envious people may voice jovial sentiments as long as they and others follow the unwritten decision not to risk being themselves.

If envious schemers adhere to a religion, they may twist the tenets of their belief system to level those around them. In past history they might have been supporters of violent inquisitions in the hope that they could detect and destroy self-motivated people. In modern times, they might promote fact-finding committees composed of conformists like themselves, consumed by the same scorn of what is unique.

The poison of envy spreads to all of one's character traits. No self-motivated person escapes for long the venom of its sting. To the warped, envious eye, each endeavor of original persons—a talk they give, a book they write, a solution they propose—is suspect. Obsessive envy may see faults, sinister meanings, heretical statements, and dangers to the masses no matter what one says to the contrary.

In the eyes of envious people, original types pollute the atmosphere everyone breathes. They contaminate the language they speak, the journals in which they write, the audiences they address, the students to whom they lecture, the congregations to which they preach. No fact-finding committee may be able to establish a link between envied persons and the evil imputed to them. Those who envy them will be more than happy to warn whoever listens to them of the dangerous influence self-motivated persons pose from morning to night.

From a factual point of view, envied speakers or teachers can prove that they did not say whatever lies have been attributed to them. Legally they are innocent. This truth paradoxically gives envious persons the ammunition they need to "prove" that precisely behind this front of decency lurks the evil. Triumphantly they bring to light what others miss: the fact that it is impossible to convict original persons of wrongdoing proves how untrustworthy they are. Their perversion leads them to do what is wrong under all circumstances and, at the same time, to cover up their tracks so cleverly that no one can convict them legally of any fault.

ENVY AND CONFORMITY

A person obsessed by envy may also be a fanatical conformist. Mere conformity is the refusal to live a life that is personally motivated. Conformists may wish to be—a plain John Doe, a perfect functionary, a clever operator, a non-assuming twirp—anything but a self-motivated person. They may want to meet important people and hold prestigious positions, but they refuse to stand for any idea that is at odds with those held by the people in power. They allow nothing self-reflective to touch them or to evoke thoughts that might cause them to explore their real motivations.

Conformists haunted by envy of originality live in fear: of themselves, of their uniqueness, of the burden of responsibility that recognition of their selfhood may place upon them. The envy of original people is not simply an opinion but a way of life. It is an obsession that makes its proponents unimaginative, inflexible, and impervious to the good sides of self-motivated persons and to any and all points of view that threaten collectivistic conformity in the private and public sphere.

To them, a problem-free society will emerge once everyone can be reduced to a blissful state of anonymity. Harmony will prevail the minute self-motivated people succumb to the criterion of homogeneity. Never does it strike them that renewal, not stagnation, is the destiny of a fully human society. The model conformists prefer is that of a well-oiled machine where everyone would reach the same height of excellence were it not for the annoying disturbances caused by people who insist on voicing new ideas or reinterpreting past assumptions.

In pursuit of this ideal society, conformists aspire to enlist the collaboration of the "rock solid," normal types they identify as such. Original persons are excluded from this mix. They already carry the label of "incorrigible" or "out for themselves." All that goes wrong in any situation is, in their opinion, due to the "sin" of self-motivation. Conformists have no time to think about the needs of their community constructively; they are too busy watching any move self-motivated persons make. They do not want to lose precious hours in pursuit of personal renewal. If something has to be done to improve society, they tell themselves it can be accomplished by the other good-willed impersonal types who will come after them. In this covert cleaning-up operation, they prepare the way for their successors. Their business is to unmask creative troublemakers, to denounce and expose them.

REVOLUTIONS AND ORIGINAL PERSONS

In periods of normalcy, self-motivated persons may stay in the background, pursuing good works while being prudently wary of evoking the wrath of envious people. In times of upheaval, the situation changes. Resolution breaks down the familiar patterns of life that kept envy at bay. One did not have to make choices concerning where one personally stood.

Society did that for them. Revolution catches them off guard. They lose their grip on what mode of behavior to emulate, but not for long. They are quick to catch what shape new patterns of conformity take.

Self-motivated persons are less fortunate. Revolution or no revolution, they remain uniquely responsible. In the beginning of these changing times, they may be hailed as an ally, praised because of their lack of identification with the status quo. Though the revolution may succeed in creating new public and social patterns, self-motivated persons remain themselves. They are not prone to identify wholly with any return to a comfortable, routinized existence. It is as impossible for them to adopt the modes of conformity now prevalent as it was for them to do so when former styles took precedence.

Impersonal people have no trouble adapting to whatever the majority wants. One stereotype is as acceptable to them as another. Not having to deal with the blessing and burden of selfhood, they have nothing to lose. In the beginning of the revolution, it may be tempting for some self-motivated types to delude themselves into thinking that this interruption of conformity points to the possibility of lasting improvement. Unwittingly, they reveal their expectations of reform in an unguarded way. While their spontaneous self-expression may be admired during the crisis of transition, after the dust settles, their naive anticipation of change may prove to be embarrassing.

Any sign of originality may cast further doubt on their capacity for leadership. Now impersonal enviers see their chance to stamp out these remnants of originality and to put themselves at the disposal of the establishment. They return to the unconscious drive to dismiss those who dare to remain themselves. As sad as it is to admit, obviously original persons can rarely claim victory; they can only try to let go of their expectations of being understood and continue to live in integrity. In times of revolution, they may allow their hopes to soar and expose their passion for change too forcefully, but this honest response only serves to make them more suspect in the minds of envious others. They forget momentarily that any show of conspicuous originality is likely to evoke the "invidious eye."

ENVY AND COLLEGIALITY

Many people engaged in educational and business enterprises, in social works and charitable organizations, boast of being, at least in name, collegial. This push for equality, where everyone's voice is worthy of being heard, is an ideal one would assume to be of benefit to any community. Collegiality on the administrative level of a group and in the personal life of each of its members appears to be a good outcome of the fight for social justice, peace, and mercy. At first glance, this commitment to the common good seems to be the best climate for the free unfolding of self-motivated persons. The prospect of freedom from the cramping views of envious others delights them. The upholding of collegiality seems almost too good to be true. Within such an atmosphere, everyone will be encouraged to become better listeners. The results will be a community that fosters mutual respect, one in which each member will be delighted when another is more original, wise, and creative than they.

Proclaiming the ideal of a collegial community is one thing; reaching it in reality is another. In some instances, it may prove to be more leveling than the forces driving more authoritative groups in the past. Much depends on the image collegial proponents have of the community and the place accorded to each of its members. When the vision of the group as a smoothly functioning machine prevails, true collegiality is not likely to be achieved. Collegiality becomes an exercise in false democratization where one person's opinion is as good as another's and where in the end the view of the majority prevails. "Politically correct" persons moved mainly by what the public wants may seize on collegiality as a way to keep self-motivated members in line. For them community means a collection of people, who operate under the implicit assumption that it is better to sacrifice a few original proposals than to risk deviating from the image of a smoothly operating machine.

Both self-motivated persons and impersonal conformists may proclaim the ideal of collegiality without realizing that they do not have the same goal in mind. Original persons believe that the community profits to the degree that it allows its members to be their best selves. The leveling majority abide by the opposite view. To them the community is a collection of workers who are basically alike and who should be able to perform the same functions in blind conformity to the opinions of the majority who, after all, have everyone's best interests at heart. The collectivity uses the veneer of collegiality to protect itself against the inferiority feelings self-motivated people may evoke in them when they refuse to rubber stamp the prevailing conclusions to which all must conform or be dubbed ambitious dreamers. In this climate, a few mavericks may be invited to say what they do not like about a proposed plan, but the majority will outvote them anyway. It is difficult to fight against a measure voted in by the group as a whole, especially when one has been allowed to have one's say.

In some cases, the tyranny of collegial opinions can be exceedingly subtle. The members may proclaim that reaching "consensus" is their ideal, but anyone who disagrees with them may be made to feel guilty and wayward. The measures taken may further diminish other practical conditions for living in fidelity to one's life call, but that point is irrelevant to those who interpret collegiality in collective terms. For them an individual is a statistical average of the traits everyone possesses. Anything beyond the usual is superfluous, eccentric, and a possible affront to the common good. The proclamation of each member's equal rights is in reality a defense of their place in the group as an average functionary, who may have his or her say within the limits set by the prevailing voices. The opinion of an individual should be at most an insignificant variation of the average feelings those in power have already voiced.

True collegiality is a consonant disposition that fosters the unfolding of each person in his or her uniqueness within the limits of a common life or task. Community is the place where the call to be self-motivated is most admired and protected. Self-motivation celebrates differences. One should never decide what a community should do before considering the people who comprise it with respect for their talents, gifts, and other qualifications. Collegiality creates an atmosphere that reverences a diversity of temperaments and traits. Enlightened by love, collegiality never leads to the suppression by a vocal majority of someone's unique-communal calling by the mystery. Mellowed and illumined by respect, each member shows sensitive concern for the call of every other member. Such patient sensitivity demands detachment from envy when a person's self-realization happens to entail endowments unavailable to others not similarly gifted. When one realizes that by background, education, and experience, he or she is not capable of wholly understanding why some persons must do what they do in the way they do it, one immediately suspends any judgmental tendency in the trust that by their fruits one shall know them.

Collegiality among people who are humble and detached is a blessing whereas without respect for uniqueness this same ideal can be devastating. The more the members of a collegial community are liberated from blind fascination with the plans they want to impose on the organization, the more likely they are to encourage each person to be their best and most creative self. Collegiality should offer the occasion to develop projects and structures that give reasonable room for the realization of originality without jeopardizing the minimum requirements for unity in the community.

A wrong view of collegiality leads one to believe that entrance into any group demands that persons sever themselves from their selfhood with its personal story line, its history, religion, world view, talents, and interests. According to this point of view, individuals are plunged into common enterprises as if they were moveable particles no different from any other. Nothing is required of a person but that he or she be a well-functioning cog in the machinery of this collegial collectivity.

Anti-originality and the envy that lurks behind it may erupt in hostility towards original persons, who refuse to surrender their selfhood. Because violent attacks are unacceptable, this feeling seeps through when envious persons indulgently declare: "The only thing I have against so-and-so is his or her lack of community spirit." Impersonal collegial types may posture good will and generosity, but they are not inclined to come to the defense of self-motivated persons. They pride themselves on being open to all sides of the situation, but they avoid any conflict that may disrupt what they call loving and peaceful sisterhood and brotherhood. They are professional peacemakers, inclined to appease anti-original types as one would quiet with condescending kindness a stubborn child. The collegial majority may profess moderation and tolerance, but they extend such dispositions mainly to those who agree with them. Their obsequious "understanding" gives them the extra room they need to erode the conditions that uphold another's self-motivated life.

Rather than feeling consoled, an original person may feel endangered when an enterprise becomes too collegial. Such an undertaking may not necessarily value dedication, personal growth, and individual dignity. It may be concerned mainly about feelings and opinions cherished by colleagues and the anonymous public. High value is placed on pleasing those in authority; on climbing the corporate or communal ladder; on doing whatever it takes not to evoke feelings of guilt, inferiority, or envy. Self-motivation is a mixed bag in such an organization.

This common misinterpretation of collegiality leads to a collective, if not a crowd, mentality. Only those who please supervisors or their peers are found acceptable. Modes of praise disguise subtle power ploys. One must please at all cost those who are on committees tasked to present blueprints for building community. The more confidence one exudes, the more approval one gains. Socializing and back-slapping may become more conducive to promotion than production, study, thought, and initiative. Anyone can excel in these areas but the dilemma facing persons who choose to remain self-motivated is that they have no choice but to permeate these same attributes with touches of their originality.

To put it mildly, it may not be the finest human beings who reach the pinnacle of success in a leveling crowd or collectivity. This place may belong to the best crowd pleaser, the obvious conformist, the smooth talker. They are the ones for whom the highest positions, and often the greatest economic compensations, may be reserved.

Obviously original persons may try to show that they, too, can play the game of impersonal conformity. Try as they might, they still have to cope with the fact that they are and will always be original characters, not "regular guys." They were pegged the moment they inadvertently betrayed their self-motivation. From then on, they became the victims of envy. No matter how hard they try to be the same as everyone else, they are not allowed to forget that they are not nor will they ever be one of the "trustworthy crowd." This is the highest accolade an impersonal collegial community can bestow on those who take pride in keeping the machinery of the homogenized collectivity running smoothly. Some of them boast about the atmosphere of loving encounter they have created, but in reality not everyone feels revered for the beauty and benevolence of their personhood.

ARMED WITH NEW SENSITIVITY

I have purposely presented in this chapter rather exceptional situations of obsessive envy and conspicuous originality not often encountered in daily life. My aim was to awaken recognition of the implicit tendency towards envy in every human heart and to depict situations in which envy may be aroused. While we may never face such extreme forms of leveling, it behooves us to catch the minute embryonic appearances of similar dynamics in ourselves and others. If an obsessive case ever crosses our path, we know what to expect.

Armed with this new sensitivity, we can now look more closely at some other appearances of envy and suggest ways in which to deal with them. Then we will be ready to take a closer look at originality and self-motivation in their usual appearances and at some of the general problems contemporary life poses to original living.

Chapter Three
Dealing With Envy

Destructive traits, readily deplored in others, are rarely recognized in oneself. While not obsessively envious, I may be prone to envy on more than one occasion. Analyzing another's motives, thinking how undeserving he or she is of compliments, harboring ill thoughts—all such episodes can be fueled by envy.

I may shy away from admitting that I feel envious since I really believe myself to be a nice, not a nasty, person. Rather than deal with the guilt it arouses, I prefer to regard it as a force outside of me. I can then analyze it as an interesting but passing phenomenon and, with detached curiosity, attribute its emergence to less polite types than myself. I may conjure up my own image of an envious person I already happen to dislike. Unfortunately, the longer I see envy only in other people, the more time it will take to learn to deal with this universal vice in myself.

To stay on the safe side and not arouse the envy of others, I may unwittingly begin to hide any sign of my own originality. The envy I might risk arousing in loved ones, friends, colleagues, and companions is then likely to be less obsessive and, therefore, easier to overcome. Remaining inconspicuous makes it less likely that my acquaintances will envy my reputation or be jealous of my career. Envy could lower their appreciation of my best endeavors, poison my friendships, and put the comfort zone in which I live at risk. I do what I can to keep it at bay, but still I cannot ignore its pernicious effects. An envious supervisor may belittle me in subtle ways. A fair-weather friend may undermine my reputation with "innocent" jokes or impute to my dedication self-centered designs. A well-meaning counselor, out of unconscious envy, may give bad advice while being fully convinced that he or she acts out of my best interests.

When we ignore the possibility of envy in people who claim to help us or in those who are close to us, we increase its potentially destructive power over us. It is wiser to ask in what way envy can affect the attitudes and actions of others towards us. Then we can deal with it more effectively.

Reflecting on envy helps us to uncover the force of this vice in our own hearts and to cope with the envy others display. When we admit to the pockets of envy in our own heart, we may begin the process of inner purification and also learn to deal with this all too common affliction in others. Then, when we happen to be the target of envy, we know from our own experience what is eating away at the person who envies us. We become vigilant in a reasonable and relaxed manner to what might ignite this feeling in him or her unnecessarily.

Such compassion may not cure the pain of envy inflicted on us by others nor may it stem its spread instantly. Neither may it prevent mean attempts to undermine our work or mar our reputation. Enlightened compassion lessens stress and leads to a better understanding of the envious leanings we may detect in those around us. Compassion clarifies our ability to spot these envious schemes before we begin to doubt what we see or question our own motives. Such understanding of the human condition makes it less likely that we will be naive victims of envious plots and intrigues. We are forewarned not to become accomplices to envy to escape loneliness or to court acceptance. To try to gain peace by complying with the envious demands of a superior, colleague, or friend is too high a price to pay. Their envy may paralyze our creativity. That being said, we must be careful not to misinterpret a reasonable demand that conflicts with our own interests as a tactic of envy.

If I happen to be an original person whose gifts reveal themselves in exceptional performance, I may be plagued by envy to the last day of my life. The tactics of envy may try to silence my voice, halt my creativity, darken my reputation. My perseverance alone may delay the victory of envy. Before I have to face the risk of defeat, I may be allowed by the mystery to accomplish something of value that expresses not only my undeserved talents but in and through them my personal values and self-motivations. There is no guarantee, however, that this respite may be granted to me. The triumph of envy may be too swift. Still, my attempt may not have been in vain. My persistence may offer some light to others—an example that reminds them to be faithful to their own initiatives in spite of detraction. Inspired by my witness of courage, they may stand up when it's their turn, willing to be counted.

When the tactics of envy endanger the effectiveness of my life and work, I need to take them seriously and deal with them wisely. I may be tempted to stop putting up any resistance simply because I want so much to be understood. In the light of amicable suggestions I receive from envious people, I may refuse to recognize the assault on what is best in me. They may never say directly that they do not want me to be different. They may not know how much they resent my expressions of self-motivations. The poison of their envy can be tucked away in attractive packages at the sight of which I am supposed to take delight. Some of these wrappings are colored by good fellowship, care for my health, concern for my sanity, virtue and name. The more poisonous the content, the lovelier the wrapping is likely to be. A trick envious people may use is to enlist me in various enterprises ill-suited to my personality or in countless committee meetings that cut unnecessarily into the time I need to pursue projects beneficial for others and more in keeping with my gifts. The wisdom of experience cautions me to be alert when abundant care begins to be bestowed upon me—all for the best; it could mean that my never-ending battle with envy has begun again.

RECOGNITION OF ENVY

To deal with envy in ourselves and others we have to be able to discern its appearances. Because its barbs are ubiquitous, all of us can recall occasions on which we've met with envy. The cruder manifestations of this malice may be locked in our memory bank; these were so blatant we cannot help but be aware of them. These were the situations in which we ourselves were the victims of envious undermining. Perhaps a person we thought we could trust turned against us out of envy and beat us out of a deserved promotion. Maybe a teacher gave us a bad grade because she was envious of our brightness or family background. Having felt the sting of envy makes it easier for us to spot its source, but this vice is not always that recognizable—neither in ourselves nor others. Envy is a master of disguise. Like pride posing as humility, it can be translated into helping others by showing them their place. For instance, when the economy is slow, we may point to the frivolous spending habits of a neighboring family booked on a holiday cruise. We boast that we have to stay home or at most visit relatives a few miles away. We claim to be practicing frugality when, in fact, we are full of envy.

The face of envy is difficult to detect because it may hide behind masks of reasonableness and modesty, wisdom and common sense. To uncover envy, recognition of its presence in and around us is an essential first step. Banning it from our hearts is the task of a lifetime. Unfortunately, there is no magic wand we can wave that will free us from this vice and its vicious tentacles. At least we can cultivate a relaxed awareness of its tactics and try not to arouse it unnecessarily. This calm sensibility may enable us to foresee the effects of envy before they escalate unnecessarily. By responding wisely to its devious ploys, we can mitigate the impact of envious words or deeds in our own life.

Recognizing the disguises of envy is important, but we still need to ponder why we tend to deny its very appearance. The truth is, we are ashamed of it. It is not nice to be envious and so we tend to conceal these feelings or call them by another name. What accounts for our shame? The answer lies in another question: What would our friends and colleagues think about us if they knew how envious we were? The shock of it keeps envy hidden within us. We disguise it from ourselves and others. Its slightest twinge sets in motion the dynamics of repression.

Let's imagine that I'm the administrator of a small business. I share my position with a person whose skill matches my own, but Jean happens to be more faithful to her originality. For many reasons, from childhood onward, I was prone to be suspicious of my own spontaneity. I came from a straight-laced family. My parents frowned upon any deed, thought, or feeling that seemed "out of bounds." Behaviors of any sort that did not correspond with their stereotyped principles of conduct were off limits.

Because I could not easily be myself, I developed an "on guard" system of defenses that interfered with the free and flexible unfolding of my skills and talents.

My associate apparently did not inherit the family inhibitions that put these subtle and overt restraints on her thoughts and feelings. Jean had the gift of being wholly present to each situation. Her involvement in the business at hand made her capable of reaching split-second decisions that were right the first time. We had the same talents and training but, unlike me, she gave her originality free play while I held my spontaneity and creativity in check. Every time we rubbed shoulders, I felt a pang of envy. If I allowed myself to admire her joyful self-presence, I fell almost immediately into envious comparison. The opposite response would have been for me to admit that in certain areas of life I was less open and friendly than my associate. Difficult as it would have been for me to make this concession, without it, envy could have escalated to the point where we might have lost a fine employee.

Having been raised in a climate where the leveling of originality is lauded as a virtue, we may be loathe to admit that others have gifts that have not been given to us. We feel envy mounting when they attain a degree of success beyond our capability of doing so. The need to feel that we have made it may be the trigger that causes us to demean their worth. Ironically, the satisfaction this tactic gives us is short-lived; it does not make us feel more certain of ourselves.

To counteract these basic feelings of insecurity, we may become workaholics who seek to outdo everyone else in production and consumption. We may purchase expensive houses, cars, clothes, and other goods as a means of announcing, "Look how indispensable I am, how much I have gained on my own, how envious others are of me!"

The insecurity that prompted this push to succeed cannot be resolved by an increase in external marks of success. Such increases may assuage temporarily the envy that eats away at one's interiority, but the "green monster" reappears as soon as another original crosses our path. We may feel compelled again to augment production and consumption, to increase rewards and recognitions, but none of these attempts guarantees the removal of ingrained envious habits. The roots of this vice cannot be removed by shrugging off our skills or demanding a better salary. What needs to be awakened are our originality and its resources complemented by deep respect for one another's dignity.

ADMITTING THAT I AM ENVIOUS

This admission may seem ludicrous if we have been led to believe that there is nothing unique about us, that we are all basically alike, and that our differences are due only to good or bad upbringing, to right timing and sheer luck. These explanations are less offensive to our ego and less threatening to our already shaky self-esteem. Despite the evidence of human originality that manifests itself above and beyond the framework of functional performance, we prefer to maintain the lie that in the last analysis nobody is better than anyone else in anything. If George had the same background as Justin, he would be as likeable and perhaps even more so. If Jean's associate had had a different set of parents, she would have been as brilliant. Envy convinces us that excellence has nothing to do with the unique-communal life call that may manifest itself through any number of aptitudes. Envy prevents us from admitting in humility that we are different from, although of no less worth than, the envied other. To the degree that we have found and accepted the hidden treasure of our own uniqueness, whether or not we express this gift in performances that are striking and impressive, we will have taken the first step to the transformation of envy into respect. If we no longer feel threatened by the originality of a family member, friend, or colleague, we can initiate an enriching interaction between us, a celebration of our mutual uniqueness. Once we acknowledge the original value we see in others, we cease feeling inferior or envious of them. We are who we are and both of us deserve to be respected.

Envy of originality cannot be disconnected from the way we feel about ourselves. Our self-esteem is connected to our call-appreciation. Only when we allow the original presence of others to lessen our own feeling of self-worth do we feel envious of them. Respect for originality leads, by contrast, to expressions of humble self-assertion of who we are called to be, no matter what we do. Though we may fail at times to be faithful to our calling, though we may never live up to it perfectly, we can come to appreciate the love of the mystery for us and extend this loving regard to others.

ENVY IN CHILDHOOD

One reason why many of us do not come to this relaxed level of self-acceptance can be traced to our childhood. As children, we develop--over and above our essential originality—a kind of "second self." Family, neighborhood, and school make us feel, think, and behave in certain ways that may be at odds with who we truly are. Deeply inculcated in us, this set of thoughts, sentiments, and attitudes may be opposed to our original gifts. Having invested this pseudo-original self with such a motivating force, we may feel compelled to totalize this structure of alien motivations, as if it constituted the whole of who we are. A sediment of external attributes of selfhood covers up the rich soil of our originality. This false self may prove to be the seedbed of envy. Instead of trusting and acting in tune with the original ground of our thoughts and actions, we substitute for our true self an imposed or quasi-originality, which may lead not only to self-envy but also to the envy of others. This false self may be set in stone by the prejudices of the society into which we are born. Our choices may be shaped more by the leveling mentality we imbibe than by respect for originality.

At the deepest level of our life we are unsure of who we are. We fight these feelings by asserting our practical and conceptual accomplishments within the culture. Every time we do something that merits the praise of others, we experience a feeling of ego-inflation. Unsure as we are of our true self, we need to boast of our achievements and have others confirm them. The insecurity instilled in us in childhood forces us to uphold this facade of originality. The expected safety zone we thought we would inhabit leads only to more uncertainty.

People who have substituted early in life a quasi-originality for their true uniqueness seem somehow to gravitate towards one another. What they share is a common ground of insecurity posing as certitude about their sense of self-worth and the secret conviction that they are the ones others ought to emulate.

EGO AFFIRMATION AND EGO-ENVY

Say I meet at a dinner party a person caught in the same web of envy in which I am entrapped. Our conversation soon moves from pleasant exchanges to play by play boasts. We tell each other about the marvelous work we have been assigned to do on a certain prestigious committee. We compare everything from our presentations to the vacations we have taken on the company credit card. We drop the names of the important people with whom we associate. Our conversation moves back and forth like a competitive tennis match. The more skillfully we play this game of mutual back-slapping, the more we reinforce each other's quasi-originality. Soon we extol the excellence of the views we share and all that we have in common. We name more acquaintances who embody our list of achievements and belittle those who have not reached these heights. A process of individual and mutual ego-inflation takes place under a veneer of polite give-and-take. These two workers cover up their envy of originality with a slew of secondary motivations, such as "telling it like it is" for the sake of unmasking those who do less than they do to serve, for instance, an impressive list of charitable and religious causes.

What is missing in this exchange is the humble self-assertion that coincides with simply being who one is. This freeing experience prevents us from playing the game of one-upmanship and from relying on the make-believe security directives it arouses.

The scene shifts when we meet a person who manifests the poise of true self-assertion and who is not at all impressed by the egocentric boasts that seem to enamor others. Remember the fairy tale of Cinderella. All she possessed was her simple, honest self. Her stepmother and stepsisters were proud of their palace, their wardrobe, their standing in society. Yet the prince, much to their amazement, falls in love with a servant girl because she is true to herself.

The unassuming originality of a character like Cinderella reminds us of the self-worth that wards off envy. We realize that competitive comparisons only cause the wound of falsehood to fester. Behind boastful behavior lurk new doubts about ourselves that become the breeding ground of envy. The spontaneous self-assertions characteristic of call-appreciation follow the opposite course of showing mutual respect and avoiding condescension or condemnation. Instead of celebrating our experiences, envy tempts us to reduce them to the level of measurable accomplishments. As a result of denying our true calling, we may find ourselves on more than one occasion disregarding our uniqueness and focusing instead on our performance in isolation from the personal originality it happens to embody and reveal. Now we are able to tell ourselves and perhaps to convince others that we could have achieved the same degree of excellence were the same educational and other advantages afforded us. We reduce original persons to the unoriginal levels of ego-envy we habitually escalate, thereby silencing the summons to be and become our true selves. Before long, we may succumb to the most telling symptom of this perversion of truth, that is to say, we begin to believe the lie that originality is due only to the "luck of the draw." This false assumption holds fast until we discover that even were we to obtain all these imagined "perks," our insecurity would not disappear. One way to come to genuine self-insight is to imagine what might happen were we to acquire the assets we now envy. Would we really feel like mature, self-motivated persons? Would we no longer be irritated by others' uniqueness?

This consideration may lead to the admission that what really arouses our envy is the fact that these persons are loyal to their calling in life and we are not. They are willing to sacrifice for the sake of their originality any ego-affirmations that clash with it, and we are not. We may come to the insight that we can never acquire this depth of originality by means of functional performance. We should cease coveting it, accept our selfhood, and be loyal to who we are. Rather than envy the traits we admire in others, we ought to emulate their affirmation of uniqueness. Once we let go of the burden of prideful boasting, we may find ways to express our newly discovered self without having to fixate on one or the other proof of our importance. When the achievement mentality ceases to be our overriding concern, envy lessens almost automatically. We respect every person who appears on the horizon of our existence because we respect ourselves. It humbles us to think what we would have missed had we allowed ego-envy to dull the inner voice of true originality.

Envy and Originality

The virtues of call-appreciation and humble self-acceptance may still be shadowed by feelings of inferiority traceable to initial formation in childhood. Persons whose gifts and talents have not been confirmed by parents or significant others are prone from an early age to engage in competitive comparisons, escalated by envy. The more they fail to differentiate who they are in their uniqueness, the more this vice may gain a foothold in their personality.

Due to their youth and lack of verbal skills, children do not yet have a well-delineated perception of who they are. As a result, envy may arise sporadically, for example, over who gets what toy, but it is not a deeply rooted personal attitude. A child may drift into situations, periods, or incidences of envy without becoming an envious person. Only if these episodes become prolonged and habitual may they point to the beginning of lasting patterns. With this reservation in mind, let us take another look at the nature of envy in childhood.

The occasions on which children experience envy may be balanced by the openings they find for mutual admiration and respect. Childhood is a time of learning from parents and others like older siblings the difference between these two dynamics. Especially because children feel so small and dependent, they look to older people to provide for their basic needs for food, clothing, and shelter. It is impossible for them to grasp until later the inner meaning of originality manifested by others. For now theirs is only a vague, rather undefinable apprehension of these parental caregivers, who are in some way the sources of all that is appreciative or depreciative in their daily life. They may sense, if no more than in a bodily way, that those older than they are can initiate changes on their own, but this capacity for self-initiation does not yet belong to them. This sense of limits may account for why children, without even knowing it, may feel envious of their parents, brothers or sisters, who seem to be able to do as they please.

What happens to children who respond to the superiority of others in their family with envy? An envious reaction may come and go whereas a more habitually envious response is like an admission that one is less than others and can do nothing about it. Such a belief may render children so inert and resentful that they may abandon any attempt to grow to a more mature appreciation of themselves and others. The more deeply rooted these tentacles of envy are, the more they preclude the possibility of admiring a once envied person. Sooner than later envious children demand the same attention, praise, rewards, rights, and privileges as others without doing anything to deserve them. Envy stymies their growth. Instead of a normal occurrence in childhood, it becomes an habitual disposition of their heart, a lifelong affliction. Children cannot wholly avoid its emergence, but they can learn from wise parents to guard against its unnecessary arousal or continuation. That is why, at the first sign of envy, parents should do all that they can to prevent its prolongation and not to allow it to become a lifelong abnormality.

Sustained envy in childhood hinders one's unfolding for two reasons. First of all, it affects the growth in respect that ought to characterize any familial or social setting. Young children need to be taught not to envy their older family members. Temper tantrums, wisely handled, teach children that they cannot acquire at once the authority granted to parental figures in their lives. Childlike respect signifies a spontaneous compliance with their parents' attempts to foster their human and spiritual growth. There is a readiness on their part to emulate the standards set for them in regard to learning everything from table manners to sharing toys. From these small lessons emerges the lifelong disposition not to be envious of the gifts they see in others but to respect the unique share that is theirs.

Secondly, an unmitigated deformative bent towards envy in childhood erodes respect for any authority, parental or otherwise. Weakened by envy is appreciation for the values honored and lived by others. Once one loses the inclination to look again in gratitude at the good one's peers and teachers do, one misses the inspiration to emulate and appropriate the joys and sufferings respectful relations bring.

For young children, emulation of the lives of admired others happens without much self-awareness and with practically no inner struggle or advanced planning. Theirs is not really a personal movement but a prepersonal orientation toward values that can be fostered or hampered by one's parents or their substitutes. Only later in life may this orientation become a personal and freely chosen attitude conducive to every level of maturation. In the absence of respect for persons worthy to be emulated, this disposition is likely to be replaced by its radical opposite, envy, which inhibits appropriation of the many invaluable skills and attitudes their parents could teach them.

As children grow older, they may become obsessed by envy if this disposition is allowed to flourish unchecked by caregivers and educators. Accompanying such blind envy may be a pre-focal, followed by an increasingly focal, refusal to appropriate the self-motivationss others exhibit in their own lives. Rebellion and resentment may replace the development of this original sense of self, first by tentative imitation of self-motivated others, and then by the discovery and unfolding of one's own uniqueness. Envy makes such healthy movements of the heart impossible.

Traceable to the disposition of envy is the delay of all forms of self-motivation in children. Later, as students, for example, they may refuse to listen to what a teacher has to say; their willful deafness may be due to envy of the originality of others, accompanied by an ostentatious display of their own aggressive attempts at ego-affirmation. Children who refuse to learn from or obey others because of envy find themselves caught in a vicious circle: on the one hand, wanting to be themselves and, on the other hand, resenting the originality shown by others in their surroundings. None of us can be our own exclusive source of growth. Children who envy others and estrange themselves from those more highly developed than they are, may alienate themselves from the very ways that would enable them to discover in freedom who they are.

Envy compels them to give up learning while pretending that they are smarter than others who refuse to lag behind. They fail to comprehend that their envy stems from a frustrating sense of their own imagined inferiority and an equally strong sense of another's imagined superiority. Increased envy makes it more difficult for them to follow the path of wholehearted emulation that might lessen the dilemma in which they find themselves and lead to their deliverance from the grip in which this vice holds them.

DYNAMICS OF CHILDHOOD ENVY IN ADULT LIFE

The dynamics of envy in childhood can reappear in adult life and further stultify our growth. I remember a student named John, who could have become an outstanding psychologist were it not for the envy that had invaded his interior life. The moment he perceived anyone as superior to him, he refused to learn anything from them. Like many an envious person, he was obsessed with becoming admired, imitated, and held up as exemplary by others. His desire was not to find his deepest self in dialogue with the values already lived by others more accomplished than he. His quest for originality was reduced to an ego project. He wanted to look original, that is to say, to be conspicuous as an inventive person, to be lauded as creative by students and colleagues. He grasped impatiently for a status that could only be his after long reflection and intense study under advanced teachers. When he encountered a truly original colleague, he could not admit to himself that this person was more creative than he. He envied him or her, although he could not admit this to himself. To do so would amount to confessing that he felt inferior to this person and to saying, "I really am his superior. I cannot stand his fake originality, yet it reminds me painfully that I may never be able to compete with such a light."

Admitting his colleague's superiority would expose him to the danger that there may be others like him who are also better than he is—teachers, writers, and speakers whose originality he can never hope to emulate. The best course to escape envy would have been for John to let go of the frustration he felt and accept with joy his own giftedness. Instead he told himself that it was only a matter of time before others saw what he did. He chose to erode his colleague's reputation for excellence by disassociating him from other renowned psychologists, saying in effect, at least to himself, "I will laud them to level him."

And so it goes with John. In all fairness, he might never say or think such things consciously. The words imagined here well up from the train of thoughts set in motion by envy. Like the vice it is, it closes him to the possibility of learning from mentors who could have benefitted his career. One professor of his was always willing to spend after hours tutoring him, but John walked away from this opportunity in favor of gathering endless reams of notes for the book he promised himself he would one day produce and "show them all." Even the few papers he did manage to write were composed in a spirit of negative identity. His goal was to point out only what this or that author forgot to say.

In the course of his study John amassed a quantity of information about human psychology but seemed unwilling to apply it to his own personality. Unfortunately, this process of envious comparison repeated itself year after year in his scholarly life. Whenever he met a teacher, supervisor, or colleague superior to him and a possible source of growth, he would fall into the same pattern of obsessive envy. He would spend all his time comparing him or her in an invidious way to other persons of fame.

I have not seen John for a long time, but it would not surprise me if he still lived entrapped by envy and unable to grow in spite of his own talents. John's deformations may echo childhood patterns of envy he has never dared to address. He may have to become a client in his own field of psychotherapy to liberate him from the net of spite in which he is caught.

COPING WITH ENVY IN CHILDHOOD

As soon as parents or significant others become aware that a child of theirs evinces noticeable envy, they should try their best to create a family situation in which he or she may feel less overwhelmed by this avalanche of spiteful resentment of the gifts of siblings or other children. Ostentatious displays of power, especially on the part of parents, ought to be avoided. Children feel threatened enough by the authority of their parents, especially when it is compounded by angry outbursts or the silent treatment. When one's parents seem unapproachable, there is a break in the natural flow of trust and respect children can show toward them. Instead they feel lost and unwanted. They may react to these feelings with envy of what their parents have but seem to withhold from them. Envy then blocks their respectful surrender to the values their parents ought to represent.

The escalation of envy in childhood may also be due to the estrangement they notice between their parents. Mother and father may be so preoccupied with their own conflicts and frustrations that they dismiss or neglect the emotional and spiritual needs of their children. They become like strangers who manifest a faraway superiority that confines itself to a tense world of their own. It is not a solution for parents to pretend that there is no conflict between them at all. Children sense the tension that hangs in the air. In many cases, one of the parents may still be able to relate well enough to the child to prevent the emergence of inferiority feelings and the envy they breed. In other cases the only solution may be for parents to seek professional help to solve their problems. Then they may be able to ease the growing obstacle of envy of self and others in their children.

Without much warning, any of us can be faced with a student, acquaintance, colleague, or employee locked in envy. Being aware of its presence may lessen the painful impact of envious disparagement we have to endure. The same insight may help us to treat others' envious tactics with a sense of empathy that makes them less inclined to escalate them. If an occasion arises when we can converse honestly about such matters and perhaps help someone to see what is troubling them, that would be splendid, but such an opportunity may not present itself. Untimely attempts on this score are likely to be met with scorn.

The question of deepest concern is: what can we do when we become aware that we ourselves suffer from this envious disposition? To even ask this question already promises some improvement. The affliction of envy is generally not available to our consciousness, so to bring it to awareness is a first step in the direction of renewal and transformation.

We may receive some inkling of our own envy when we see its dynamics magnified in unusual cases. Once we spot even the smallest symptom we should reflect on it in a relaxed way, disclosing in what measure it may apply to us. Reflection makes us sensitive to the emergence of envy in our everyday life. In the beginning we may discover only a few isolated and seemingly unrelated events. Then the evidence mounts. After a period of patient observation, we may detect the emergence of an envious pattern.

We may begin to see how it has stunted our growth and eroded our peace of mind. We may be motivated to work through this pattern of envious isolation, gradually liberating ourselves from it.

As always, the confirming companionship of a wise and compassionate friend may be the key to relieving us from the distress of envy. Helpful in severe cases may be therapy or counseling or certain types of group dynamics, conducted under professional supervision. Members of the group may point out how isolated and uncommunicative we are when we demonstrate unwittingly a sampling of our envious behavior in their presence.

CHILDREN ENVIED BY PARENTS

A case in which the roles are reversed happens when instead of children envying their parents, parents envy a gifted child. Successive generations of a family plagued by envy may be at the root of this dangerous tendency. If the current generation does not find a solution for it, envy may stretch into the next generation like links in a chain. How does this transference come about?

It is certainly not true that we inherit envy. Neither do we learn directly these inner envious responses to people who appear superior to us. We may learn from envious others how to speak disparagingly about people seen as superior to us, but that does not mean that we follow the pattern of envy with its condescending sentiments and uncomplimentary perceptions.

Parents obsessed by an envious attitude towards others may direct it at a child who refuses to be like everybody else. When he or she shows a quality his or her parents have belittled in others, they are only too ready to belittle it in them.

I remember a man whose brothers and sisters went through college successfully. Afterwards they did well in various fields. He himself was less brilliant during his high school years. He was a mediocre student, but still he could have made college if he had tried a little harder. A college degree would have been for him the key to a moderately successful life in the professional world. However, he was so envious of the brilliance of his brothers and sisters that he felt compelled to deny the value of education and the usefulness of learning. To spite them and the whole hated world of educated people, he left high school in anger. He refused to prepare himself for anything other than a low-paying menial job. He married a woman caught in the same envious preoccupation. They had a child who showed a natural brightness, a spontaneous interest in learning. Not surprisingly, she aroused the envious attitude of her parents. They debunked her attempts to better herself educationally. They spoke disparagingly of her well-educated aunts and uncles. Their reaction bewildered the child. It interfered with her self-discovery. To believe and follow her parents meant that she had to falsify her own interest in learning and to forgo the love for books she felt so strongly. She submitted to the view of her parents. She began to imitate their ego-inflated insinuations. It was not long before their envious dispositions sunk into her own heart.

To be sure, this story could have ended differently. She could have found other people to follow, such as one of her disparaged uncles or aunts. To expect such an independent choice on the part of a vulnerable child may be asking too much. One way to help persons who are the victims of such a distortion in childhood may be to present them with the chance to rediscover their own gifts before they are veiled by the envious orientation of their parents.

OBVIOUSLY ORIGINAL CHILDREN IN A LEVELING SOCIETY

A child may be so original that no amount of leveling in the family can erase his or her spontaneity. Their uniqueness shows itself, moreover, in unusual interests, behaviors, and pursuits. Rather than evoking admiration, such children may become early in their lives a point of curiosity and an object of envy, placing before them a never-ending series of challenges if they are to develop properly.

Children in a leveling society are raised to adjust themselves, no questions asked, to its demands. The same leveling arena allows for some standard rebellion among adolescents as long as it stays within bounds: "Teenagers will be teenagers!" The subculture that rebels shows in its structure the same features as the homogenizing society as a whole.

Children may be defiant as a group, but woe to the gifted child or adolescent who dares to be him or herself in an original way within the group.

Let's say the rebellious group of boys and girls likes rock music. The moment a member of the gang dares to let on that he likes classical music, too, he exposes himself to being branded a "square." The gang likes noisy togetherness at every moment of the day; she sometimes prefers solitude and reads books the other girls find stupid. Soon she stands silently condemned. When in his conversation he offers another view of music, his peers remind him that he'd better get with the program. When she tells the girls about an inspiring novel, they look at her and snicker smugly. Why does she have to be so out of it?

She begins to feel apart from them, not a part of her age group. She may not be insensitive to their interests. She might even want to be like them in every way, but she cannot. It is not a matter of feeling that she is better or worse than they are but of knowing that she is different. The other youngsters seem to be more accepted by peers and parents than she is; they are not considered "oddballs." They never seem disturbed by original thoughts, feelings, and dreams. Yet, strangely, they are said to be interesting while she strikes others as a dud. This aspect of her reputation may always remain a mystery to her. Why do they find these kids so fascinating? What do they see in them that she does not have?

Many inner and outer upheavals may occur when a child discovers her reputation as an obviously original person in a leveling society. This discovery sets her apart from the "normals" in her circle and the reason is not simply attributed to her originality. Other youngsters may be as original and self-motivated as she. What makes her originality obvious—and hence irritating—are the rather exceptional interests and talents through which it shows itself and about which she can do nothing. Some relief from this confusion may be found when she meets an understanding teacher or friend who encourages her to be grateful for her gifts and explains the unwritten rules of reasonable adaptation. Her mentors may make sure that her expressions of originality are not yet perverted by the stereotypes of a pragmatic society. With many people she may feel like an outcast but not with those rare understanding persons, who help her to sense that she is "in" with humanity on a deeper level. Still, no matter what she says or does, her reputation for originality like her love for reading follows her. When the pain of being different becomes too great to bear, disrespectful, envious voices may grow louder and remind others: "That's what you'd expect such an oddball to do." Posturing serious concern, they might add, "She would have been just fine if she had been like the other kids and kept her nose out of those books."

Forgotten by such leveling claims is that no one should be an exact copy of anyone else. These children did not ask to bear the weight of originality, but there is no way they can deny their destiny. Compassion, not derision, is the best way to prevent these unnecessary stresses on their physical, emotional, and spiritual well-being.

In the worst case, educators or other authority figures may compound the misunderstanding already incurred on their journey. They themselves may be representatives of the functional society, who believe that perfect adjustment, achieved by leveling uniqueness, is a guarantee of success.

Resisting such an array of unoriginality can be incredibly stressful. For exceptional children, the only alternative may be a flight from the leveling process into a more or less isolated existence, but this is not the wisest course to follow. Dealing with envy without becoming embittered is a challenge not everyone can meet. It is best facilitated when one remains appreciative of one's own and others' originality despite the depreciative types that try to discourage fidelity to their calling. Maturity in this matter may irritate those who feel superior to them, especially in the realm of functional interaction, practical adjustment, regular fellowship, sports and public debate, but just because they happen to be better in these areas is no excuse for envy.

Faced with the ambiguous attitudes of others towards any expression of their uniqueness may lead one to invent modes of adaptation that temper or prevent these jolting reactions. Experience shows that paranoid attitudes like anxiety and false guilt isolate them more than necessary from their companions. Being flexible to begin with, one may develop a style of life faithful to one's originality and its acceptable manifestations without attracting undue attention and the envy and jealousy that may accompany it. Such an adaptive approach to reality can stop the poisonous spread of depreciation and protect one from a loss of gentleness.

Original types will always be faced with a two-fold task. First, they must reflect on the envious life situations in which they find themselves. They need to discover how they can live with the least detriment to themselves and others. Secondly, they must consider the ineffective attitudes which they developed in childhood to cope with envious people. They must ask themselves: "What are the effects of my childhood experiences and my reactions to them? How can I change my life in such a way that I will be less in conflict with others?"

ENVY IN THE SOCIAL DEVELOPMENT OF CHILDREN

Normal incidents of envy happen regularly among children. This kind of envy is universal in their social development and that of society. Envy as such does not teach children compassion for the pain it evokes in others. It certainly does not help the envied child to come to inner harmony and relaxed self-discipline. How, then, does childhood envy make a contribution to one's socialization?

At the root of beneficial social behavior is a mature motivation to care for others out of love and respect. The implementation of this motivation in daily life demands relational skills that in themselves can be used for social as well as anti-social purposes. A good example of one such skill is the art of diplomacy. I can be diplomatic in a genuine attempt to foster better relations with others. Diplomacy can be abused as well for selfish purposes. Clever diplomats may use this skill only to enhance their position at the cost of another's downfall.

In the case of envy of originality in childhood, a striking example can be found in one of the skills necessary for societal comportment, in a word, self-control. One can be taught to avoid words or deeds that arouse envy in others. Children can develop self-discipline in regard to original expressions that may irritate those around them unnecessarily. Circles of family members, friends, and acquaintances, near and far, benefit from such courteous behavior. Showing off one's expressions of originality at the expense of less talented others is always impolite. This type of sensitive socializing offsets the emergence of irresponsible individualism.

Prudent controls of a personal and social nature may begin to be developed in childhood to celebrate, not demean, one's own and others' expressions of originality. Children envious of its attractive manifestations in some of their peers may still try to keep these feelings within the bounds of respect for and acceptance of diversity. This practice leads to a lessening of prejudice and the leveling mentality it breeds. Children who have not learned to control their envy may devise alone and in company unjust coping mechanisms like ridicule, disapproval, and rejection of others—all of which diminish the risk to be original. People treated in this way become cautious. They are reluctant to show their spontaneity; they force themselves to play the role that wins them favor. They may even start to mock their own self-motivation, however modestly it manifests itself.

The development of inner warning signals to ward off envy may happen early in the life of talented children. They do whatever it takes to avoid arousing the envy of siblings and playmates. They feel the invidious eyes of envy upon them every time they experiment with expressions of their own originality. Sooner than later they acquire skills that can be used for legitimate self-protection. More mature children may become motivated to keep their originality in check out of compassion for those less in tune with their selfhood and less able to express it through the undeserved gifts they have received. They try to avoid hurting others by tempering words and actions that are sure to arouse envy if they are not held in check. In this case, their skill of self-control arises not from a defensive, protective posture but from their care and concern for those around them.

As long as anxiety about the envy of others remains the only source of self-discipline, it can become a repressive force in regard to one's own self-emergence. Its effect will be negative. Healthy development is characterized by a transition from control of the expression of originality out of fear to its temperance out of respect for oneself and others. One learns not to evoke envy by showing off one's gifts but to bear with the envy that is unavoidable as long as one tries to be true to him or herself. The first act implies candor, the second courage.

MITIGATION OF ENVY AND EXPRESSIONS OF ORIGINALITY

The various patterns of envy and of being envied, which may develop in our life, together with possible ways of ameliorating their painful consequences, do not cancel the fact that we will always have to bear the hurt envy evokes. Loyalty to our own originality, especially when its expression tends to be rather exceptional, means that no matter what we do we will not be able to escape this suffering. We can only hope to mitigate it by accepting in serenity that in a leveling society to have the good reputation of being original may be seen as more threatening than transforming.

Still an original person must learn to live with his or her original-ity in as tranquil a way as possible. Such serene acceptance lessens the hold envy may have on our own heart. Vigilance is appropriate, but that is no excuse to deform our character by unnecessary anger, aggres-siveness, or defensiveness in response to any barbs of envy we may have to endure.

Envied persons must not merely survive in society. They must develop an harmonious rhythm between avoidance of envy and acceptance of its tenacity as a capital sin. To be ourselves in an envious society means that we must live a life of contrasts, veering between caution and compassion. To be faithful to who we are, we must seek solitude without isolation and communion without the loss of privacy. We must not imagine we can always duck the blows of envy, but we must try to shy away from words and deeds that evoke it unnecessarily. While not being unduly preoc-cupied with our own reputation, we must remain concerned for all those whose life may be linked to ours. What envy does to us, it can do to those around us, who may not be ready to bear with this kind of detraction. For others' sake, we must often be satisfied with living a hidden life among our peers, maintaining discretion and silence about our personal accomplishments and creative enterprises. Such vigilance must at one and the same time foster the sobriety of contemplation and the spontaneity of effective action.

Impossible as it may seem to execute these dual directives, we must try to do what we can to live as original persons in an unoriginal world, neither succumbing to the tyranny of a collective mentality nor becoming embittered because we are not always understood. The answer is not to withdraw from life in an attempt to be faithful to ourselves on some fantasy island freed from envy but to respect its reality and respond not in kind but with respect.

To live in harmony with the demands of my original commitment depends in great measure on the way I respond to the people, events, and things I meet along the way. I can adapt my style of living to my surroundings, at least to some degree, without compromising my originality. Having a generous heart has to become an indelible part of my personality. It is the outward expression of the inward disposition of appreciative abandonment to the mystery.

If I am an outgoing person by temperament, my style of giving usually exudes a thoughtful balance of firmness and gentleness. When admonition is warranted, I express my concern with a smile. The same generosity of spirit prevails in every situation. The social component of this virtue alerts me to good causes that merit my support as well as to unjust actions that call for critique. I adjust the means and manner of my giving accordingly. The way I express my generosity changes in the light of my compassionate commitment to adapt to the needs of others. Envy has no place in this pursuit of virtue. I pay respectful attention to others' requests and do all that I can to enable them to live a better life physically, mentally, emotionally, and spiritually.

Consider a college student who wants to show her generosity in social action. She volunteers for work as a lay associate of a missionary order, giving to others without sparing herself. In spite of her efforts to adapt, many of the people she serves find her temperament rather stand-offish and cool. They dub her a "typical Yankee." She feels hurt. After all, she did not come so far for the fun of it. She came to help those in need. At home in New England, people had ridiculed her for her exaggerated generosity. Now she realizes that she can only serve others effectively in this part of the world if she puts more warmth than wariness into her style of social care. After some time the latter disposition becomes second nature to her. She overcomes the antipathy others felt when they first met her. Although she cannot match their exuberance, she finds that this is not what the people expect of her. It pleases her and them that the genuine feelings of generosity she has begun to radiate flow into the rest of her behavior. When the time comes for her to return to the United States, her parents and friends comment on how much she has changed. Happily for her, the expression of originality in one dimension of her life has affected her character formation as a whole.

The same principle of adaptive living can be applied to each person's life. We have no choice but to live as original persons in a functionalistic society. Our skills in self-expression have to include the art and discipline of being attuned to the way in which average citizens look upon any unique person in their midst. We need to be able to express our originality without arousing undue envy. The treatment we receive and give ought not to be a threat to anyone. Originality thrives in a climate of equanimity where we respect our differences as well as the kinships we may feel. When envy happens anyway, we must try within reason to erase the false picture others have painted of who we are, all the while realizing that perfection in this regard is not within our reach.

While extraordinarily gifted artists, musicians, and philosophers like Leonardo Da Vinci, Amadeus Mozart, and Søren Kierkegaard may have enjoyed public and professional esteem in the long run, in their lifetimes they knew the pain of depreciation by less gifted people, who labeled them conceited show-offs whose productions would never last. Their experience illustrates what can happen to all of us on a smaller scale. Others may impose on us a reputation we do not recognize in ourselves, but it only further demeans us to react to this misperception in a hostile manner. To attempt to associate only with our own kind in an exclusive community to which others will never be admitted only serves to confirm the suspicions of those who envy us already. Original persons only add to the ordinary alienation they may at times feel by becoming the "strange birds" others predicted they would be. The tight association they formed to protect them from envy further stymies their deepest desire to be of service to others. Being original persons in an unoriginal society is hard enough without arousing the suspicion of the anonymous public.

The temptation to respond in this isolationist manner is difficult to resist. The depreciative labels others apply to any sincere expression of originality are not easily shaken off in a leveling society. They emerge simultaneously with the technological streamlining of a culture for the sake of functioning more efficiently. Until we learn how to balance efficiency with respect for uniqueness, we must do what we can to create conditions more favorable for rediscovering the distinctive core of our personhood. While we have no choice but to counter the leveling mentality that accompanies an automated society, we must still try to be patient with the slow pace of progress that replaces envy with respect.

DILEMMA OF ORIGINAL PERSONS IN THE PRESENT AGE

The dynamics of envy of originality are so intense that faithfulness to one's calling may arouse guilt feelings in those who have forsaken their own potential for true personhood. When impersonal types see someone who is loyal to his or her originality, they may be reminded of what they have lost. To silence the irritating voice of self-reproach, they may go on the attack. In that case, envy becomes aggressive. Its target may be those who pursue their dreams and who choose, despite opposition, not to abandon the direction of their lives to demands made upon them by envious others. What if we are not willing to pay the price of coming to this depth of self-awareness? What if we do not live up to our potential? The alternative may be to become envious people ourselves. We no longer walk in the truth of who we are; instead we work to repress these persistent inspirations. The result may be that we lash out angrily at those who have stayed true to their call solely because we see in them the liberated self we could have been.

A buffer zone to this downward spiral to envy of originality may be found in a truly humane community that offers everyone a chance to enjoy some freedom from bleak conformity and homogenized living. The path to respect for uniqueness may be cleared by the encouragement of self-motivation and original expression. The freedom thus gained moves us away from thoughtless identification with whatever public pulsations are prevalent at the moment. We welcome openings for personal growth. We resist any temptation to level others and remind them that living an original life will always be a challenge. A loving community prevents the isolation that is pernicious for self-motivated persons. In such an atmosphere, the expression of our originality is not a distant dream but a workable reality.

This adaptive decision to flow with what makes us more acceptable to others, without robbing us of our uniqueness, prevents undue arousal of their envy. Adaptation makes it possible for us to respect those with whom we have to live and work while remaining faithful to our originality. This disposition makes us more sensitive to the thoughts and feelings of our peers and colleagues. We learn how to be faithful to ourselves among others, seeking points of unity amidst our differences. The fruits of adaptation are not gained by taking motivational courses or memorizing instructional manuals but by trying to live with people in respectful empathy. We begin to *feel* into the attitudes and behaviors that might alienate us from them unnecessarily. Through observation of our own modes of presence and action, we became more acceptable to them and they to us. Following this path honors our originality without raising the expectation that others will always understand its particular expressions. A side benefit of such empathy is that it leads to forgiveness of our faulty childhood reactions against those who might have made us more prone to suffer from envy at home, in school, and in the neighborhood.

OVERCOMING ENVY BY VALUE RADIATION

While a remote control device is an object we can manipulate at will, our deepest humanity is more like a window opening us to hitherto unknown horizons. Our distinctively human transcendence dynamic enables us to go beyond the mundane routines of everyday life without leaving them behind, to function well without losing our longing for the "More Than." Through this window we behold the hidden splendor of ordinary occupations. We look at ourselves and others with respect, not resentment, we choose to embody the dispositions that diminish the dynamics of envy.

To practice the appreciative abandonment option is to remain attentive to the ultimate goodness, truth, and beauty of life. We opt to embody these essential values and we witness to their efficacy in our life and our surroundings. What interferes with this embodiment of respect, what makes envy a possibility, is any depreciation of the transcendent in our here-and-now situation. Although this option for respectful empathy may never be perfect, we can work daily to improve our responses to and our expressions of originality. While we cannot change the innate limits of our personality nor alter the current context for self-expression, we can foster just noticeable improvements (JNI's) in our outlook on life to ameliorate envy. What counts is not our success but our willingness to try. When all is said and done, we can find peace only when we accept ourselves and others as we are—limited persons called to love and serve one another as long as we live in this world. With that as our goal, we can reconcile ourselves to the fact that we may see the fruits of these human and Christian ideals in some relationships but not in all.

A certain tension arises in our attempts due to two conflicting characteristics. On the one hand, it seems as if we now gravitate toward those values we experience as contributing to our growth in empathy and adaptation. On the other hand, we know we can only concretize them in limited ways.

We continue to experience some coercive movements in the opposite direction. Still, by looking for signs of improvement, we prevent undue discouragement.

The tension between the values we live and those we desire to embody does not go away entirely, but at least it does not lead to gross outbreaks of envy of self or others. Overcoming envy by value radiation is no longer an unreachable goal but a reality. The more we flow with the waves of self-insight emerging from our unique-communal life call, the more they tell us to what degree we can live original values without evoking envy. Its shadow only emerges when we refuse to acknowledge either our gifts or our limits. It is never helpful to look spitefully on any realization of value we cannot yet live. If envy has its way, it can destroy not only our potential to radiate this value but the very value itself.

Respect—the counterpoint to envy—can also be viewed in the light of these two interacting characteristics. First this virtue is the bridge to our orientation to all that is good and true and beautiful in life; second it reminds us that to realize these gifts is an ongoing endeavor that only succeeds in limited ways. While we may experience the fruits of appreciative living; we do not always tend to embody them nor do we feel thankful when we see them manifested in others. We may not yet be ready to combine our attraction to them with our radiation of them in the culture.

Respect brings to light the originality that may lie dormant in us and others; it peels away the cataracts of envy from our eyes and results in admiration of the hidden splendor embedded in people, events, and things. We know from experience how difficult it is to detect the traces of the mystery that lie concealed under envious distortions and prejudicial perceptions. Respect lets us see who and what is really there. It returns us to the wellsprings of faith, hope and love. We believe that every human person is a revelation of value, no matter how obscure it may be. We hope that we will be granted the gift of glimpsing the inherent worth and dignity of each human life despite the woundedness due to original, personal, and social sin. We remind ourselves in love that the values we celebrate come from our participation in the Source of all that is good.

Virtues like obedience (listening to reality); poverty of spirit (letting go of our possessiveness); and chaste respectful love protect us from turning our attempts at value radiation into sterile manipulations of reality aimed at embellishing our own puffed up sense of self-importance. Such a perversion of respect puts us at risk of seeing ourselves and others through the narcissistic window of "what's in it for me?" To change course we need to admit humbly that the values we revere and hope to radiate are much greater and more mysterious than the part we play in their epiphany.

Reducing virtues to means of advancement is an exercise in arrogance that cannot inspire awe. Like an amputated part of a body or the cut-off branch of a tree, so virtue that loses contact with its nourishing ground in the mystery, remains only a passing fancy. We can adorn the branch, but without the tree, it loses its aliveness.

The attempt to accumulate values as if they were collectible items leads to envy. We greedily eye them as objects we can hoard; we are envious of those who own more of them than we do. Envy thrives in a civilization that has lost touch with the values that move individuals and groups to expressions of self-giving love and service. Respectful appreciation quells envy and lets us admire revelations of originality, no matter where or in whom they appear. No longer do we experience other persons as threats to our advancement; we know that we have been called, each in our own way, to participate in the goodness, truth, and beauty of all that is. To see these lights manifested in others now becomes our delight. Never more are they the object of our demeaning looks and spiteful stares.

Chapter Four
Self-Motivation and Originality

The fear of being who we are may cause us to go along with popular opinions we do not really share. Fear is a crippling force that attacks us both when we are awake or asleep. A nightmare a friend of mine had shows why: "I am driving a car. I gather speed. A child appears on the road. I press the brake. The car continues to accelerate. I break out in a cold sweat. I panic. It feels as if I won't be able to stop the car. At that moment I wake up terrified. The dream is so real it takes time to realize I'm in bed. My fear subsides and I breathe normally again." We converse calmly for a while and then I ask my friend if he thinks there is a meaning to the dream.

"I must have been five years old when my father took the family to a seaside resort. I enjoyed playing in the sand, but he said I needed to learn to swim in the ocean. I feel so scared of the foaming water. He walks me past it and tells me to let go of his hand. I don't dare to do so. I want to feel the safety of the sand bar, but he picks up my feet and tells me to paddle freely as I do in our pool at home. A welcome waves carries me to shore and I'm too afraid to try it again."

A swimmer who knows the sea and trusts his or her own skill loves to dive into waves. A fearful child does not trust the water. He only goes against his fear of what might happen to him if he has no choice but to follow orders. He wants to stop his swimming lesson but cannot do so.

Another person who came to talk to me was a demolition expert, who had to defuse a bomb on the verge of exploding during his tour of duty in the Army: "One wrong move and I'd be blown to bits. My instinct was to run away, but I had to force myself to do the job. It demanded convincing every muscle in my body to do what had to be done since I felt crippled by fear. I did not know if I would be killed or not, but I had to fulfill my mission. Fearful or not, I had to trust other soldiers on the team to guard me but not to interfere with my expertise."

Fearful people often give in to the goading of others. We may want to linger in the lobby of the theater, but the crowd of movie-goers pushes us toward the street. We go along with them without thinking about it. By contrast, there are times when we are more in control and able to envision our moves before we make them. The rescuer who dives into a dangerous river does not do so to prove himself but to help a drowning person. The soldier who disarms an explosive shell wants to save the lives of others, not look like a hero to win a promotion.

We may be responsive to motives that well up from within or only come from a set of "oughts" we derive from others. Teenagers who take part in the mischief of a gang may not be motivated by their own decisions but driven by the dictates of their peers. Many of us are like the members of that gang. Afraid to be the origin of our own actions, we let ourselves be swayed by the trends dictated by an anonymous public. Secretly regretting this betrayal of our selfhood, we may envy those who act on the basis of their own initiative. They make us aware of what we know on some level that we miss.

SELF-MOTIVATIONS ACCOMPANIED BY ANXIETY

Anxiety—real or imagined—weakens self-motivation. Although we may allow others to influence us too much, we have to ask at some point: "Why am I doing this and what does it mean to *me?*" Decisions of lasting importance are those we ought to make—not the crowd and not the collectivity. Self-motivation emerges from personal insights and choices, not from worrying about what others think. My original self signals where I must go and what I must do.

An animal cannot be self-motivated; neither can it lead an original life nor freely choose one meaning over another. Its instinctual make-up lets it adapt to the changing face of its environment. Its more or less fixed instincts, especially for survival, arouse it to action. There is no choice but to obey.

By contrast, self-motivations shapes human life. We may choose to do one task and omit others, for example, to eat and then decide to diet. An old friend of mine knew already as a child that he wanted to be a concert pianist. No one had to tell him to practice. He took music lessons, gave recitals, and avoided habits that might detract him from his first commitment. These and similar self-motivated acts shape us day by day. Such directives provide focal points for both our uniqueness and our communal obligations. My friend encouraged my lifelong love for classical music. Every time we saw one another, we discovered new ways in which our aesthetic tastes melded together.

At one point in his career, my friend faced an interesting dilemma. He accepted the invitation from a leader of his political party to sponsor a concert to raise money for a good cause: "His ideals to make this a better world, his rhetorical gifts and leadership skills motivated me to support him." The concert was a grand success and he could have accepted a series of commitments, but he had to take stock of his motivations: "How might this expenditure of time and energy affect my musical career?" As much as I relished the excitement of political involvement, I made the decision to support the campaign financially but not to be a major player.

Here is an example of how insufficiently appraised engagements become enlightened and guided by original insight and choice. Motivations stemming from inner appraisals spark the actions that help us to ponder the direction our life ought to take. In a sense we go where our motivations lead us. The more we listen to them, the less envious of self and others we are likely to be.

The history of humanization is the story of how to transform blind absorption in lower drives and public opinions into fully appraised directives. To the degree that this process of discernment originates in our unique self, it becomes an affirmation and expansion of our innate originality. When we are self-motivated, we channel our drives in directions that are more in tune with our gifts and limits. Accompanying this quest to combine inspiration and incarnation are the red flags of anxiety, insecurity, and envy. These flare ups of our dissonant self happen at decisive moments when we have to move beyond blind drives to new levels of self-insight and the freedom of choice that accompanies them. To elevate mere emotionality to motivation, we have to distance ourselves from worrisome distractions and become more at home with who we are. The coercive security directives that plagued us prior to this liberating event lose their binding power. We are no longer content to move where others say we should go with no consideration of our calling. Neither are we prone to let our lower needs and instincts take precedent over our higher quest for freedom from forces alien to the self we want to cultivate. It should not surprise us that the latter choice might make us an object of envy, but neither should it deter us from being faithful to our call. We accept before the Sacred the responsibility to marry or stay single, to become a political activist or join a community of pacifists, to dedicate our time to study or find our niche in manual labor. Like all original endeavors, this orientation to the whole and Holy entails the risk of stepping into the unknown.

Often our character formation stops in midstream because we do not dare to stand alone in the stark recognition that no one can make such choices for us. This effort to listen to the mystery of our call is the origin of the direction we begin to foresee as an ideal way to fulfill our vocation and avocations; it becomes the ground of decision and action; it lessens anxiety and the danger of self-envy. We accept to live in line with the values we now affirm as essential for our personal and social growth.

Imagine the effect this way of living has on a person who grew up in a climate of racial prejudice. The new insights one has acquired convince him or her to go against the grain of their upbringing and admit that racism is a serious sin eroding the equality in dignity all people share. This realization emerges from the center of one's original self: "I cannot say for sure where it will lead, but I already see the breakup of old patterns of disrespect. I have to take the risk that such a reform may alienate me from family, friends, and neighbors. At first the decision to motivate myself in this direction was fraught with anxiety. This does not surprise me. My own relatives questioned my motivations and resented me for disrupting their sense of order in society. Obstacles to change were strewn on my path like potholes on an otherwise well-paved road but none of them blocked my way. I refused to be a racist anymore!"

Even if the motivations alive in society match my own, I still have to live them in an original way. To minimize the courage it takes to change in favor of staying in the safety zone of being "politically correct" can lead to the paralysis of self-motivation. A change of this sort necessitates conversion of heart as well as a shift away from racist ways of thinking and acting that may affect further change in the economy, the school system, and the nature of law enforcement.

Motivational movements of this magnitude mean the disappearance of the familiar world we once knew and can send shock waves through a culture. Some suffer more than others because they feel themselves to be responsible agents of this transformation. Others may fight tooth and nail to maintain the status quo. They may not reach the stage of self-motivation that puts the anxiety associated with change aside and permits cultural transitions to take place. Still others opt to move *from* inadequate current forms of life *through* anxious apprehension of the implications of needed reform *to* the new world of freedom from fear that awaits them.

MOTIVATIONAL CHALLENGES IN OUR AGE

In a world where people can retire to their rooms and confine communal relations to chatting on the internet, the danger of walling ourselves off in enclaves of our own making is not to be taken lightly. We may not even know the names of our own neighbors. The unforeseen consequences of such a high degree of alienation can lead in the long run to the "quiet desperation" lived by the "mass of men" the philosopher Henry David Thoreau described in his reflections on Walden Pond. Today's society encourages us to put our career plans in place before we ponder their consequences. We prefer to anesthetize ourselves with false bravado bred by worldly success rather than face the inevitable questions evoked by fidelity or infidelity to our origin in the mystery. When we succumb to the ease of letting the anonymous public make our decisions for us, we forfeit the right to choose our destiny. Dictators depend on this relinquishment of personal autonomy. They abuse their power and make choices for their people. They substitute for a culture of life the escalation of weapons of mass destruction and suppress the human rights upheld by dissenting voices.

The more self-motivation we experience, the heavier may be the burden of truth we have to carry. Life or death may hang in the balance based on the choices we make. The illusion that we can behave with impunity never pays off. We have to be willing to accept the consequences of our decisions. Lacking a sense of personal responsibility, we may end up being victims of a world that promotes envy and precludes originality.

A surgeon performing a delicate operation on a person's heart knows his field, but he cannot foresee unknown factors beyond his control. He cannot rely on technology the way witch doctors of old relied on magical incantations. Any move we make into unchartered territory causes us to feel some fear. Each new differentiation we make at the moment means that we have to integrate our actions with what we already know and with what we think may happen. How much or how little ought we to risk making a move in response to the many courses of action open to us? What if we make the wrong decision? We must give up some certitude each time we change course. We may feel motivated by our originality to follow a directive that has not yet proven to be effective, but we cannot keep our motivational life alive unless we can bear with some degree of incertitude.

The understandable fear that accompanies original living cannot be subdued by technical know-how and organizational skills alone. In this light a leap of faith is unavoidable. Any move we make entails the expansion of motives that in the past also aroused apprehension. The range of scientific and technological progress confronting us today brings us face to face with problems we would not have dreamt of a century ago. We must ponder how to protect the dynamics of originality in a world where the accelerating pace of change has arisen to dizzying proportions.

WORLDLY COMPLEXITY AND ITS EFFECTS ON MOTIVATION

Bombarded as we are by ideas and innovations that expand our horizons of choice, we may feel like adolescents on the verge of a world waiting to be renewed. We challenge, as youngsters do, the authority figures and traditions handed down to us from former generations. This phasic upheaval, exciting as it may be, is also anxiety-evoking. The opening up of unexpected vistas prompts feelings of elation and uncertainty, of fascination and fear.

At such moments, it is tempting to prolong the indecisive bliss of adolescence. Persons in this age bracket are still under the protection of family, school, and society; they are not yet exposed to the necessity of translating their dreams into the laborious routines of everyday reality. They sense that moving towards adulthood will necessarily remove them from the certitude and safety of the past. They realize that the price of originality is the loss of unquestioned embeddedness in hearth and home. At this point of passage to maturity, they have to decide to stand with or to go against the crowd, to walk alone or to cooperate with those wiser than they who want them to succeed in their quest for meaning.

In today's world, we cannot base our motivational life on the monolithic views earlier generations once knew. In the modern era, developments in the sciences have enabled explorations beyond the confines of the earth. Inventive means of communication and industrialization have resulted in astonishing advances that tore apart the one-dimensional perspective of what it meant to be a person in the world. The advances made in pluri-traditional cultures are so revolutionary that we hardly have the time to assess them. Telescopes enable us to travel to the far reaches of the universe. Microscopes let us penetrate into the fascinating world of cellular biology. Astronauts envision landing on the planet Mars. Archaeologists reach back into time and calculate the age of the earth. Anthropologists study the emergence of humankind in the hope of unearthing the origin of the species. These scientists keep saying that the era of discovery has only just begun. The end seems nowhere in sight.

The meaning of life appears so much more complex than our ancestors suspected. The world view they took for granted in the Renaissance shattered after the Age of Enlightenment. Shocked and bewildered, we soon discovered that what people of the past believed was like a fairy tale is now in the realm of conclusions reached by the empirical and experiential sciences that are poised to explore all domains of reality.

With this expansion and deepening of knowledge comes a new wave of anxiety. Simply because we have the means to do something like, let us say, the cloning of a species, the question arises: "Ought we to do it?" The motivation to explore unknown territory now has to differentiate itself into choices as to what would or would not yield humane results. The enthusiasm to experiment is there, but the morality of one's choice cannot be overlooked. What pushes people forward may not be the rightness or wrongness of what they want to do, but their fear of not producing noticeable results. At this point, the power of envious comparison may erode the pros and cons of ethical choices. The pressure to succeed at any price may be too strong to resist. True originality lets us take another stance. We may be willing to work for a lifetime without ever seeing the successful outcome of our endeavors. Our faith assures us that we are called to be self-motivated persons whose original expressions may evoke envy in some undiscerning eyes and grateful appreciation in others.

PROBLEM OF PUBLIC ADULTHOOD

As we pass beyond the adolescent phase of human development to a not yet achieved adulthood, we enter a kind of second adolescence, fraught with problems of its own. Adolescents often find themselves in opposition to adults. They feel more at ease with their own age group and the security of familiar surroundings. Adults are more comfortable with the idea that society has to be organized in accordance with already established patterns. This thought never crossed their minds as adolescents. Now they realize that their success depends at least partly on their willingness to go along in some measure with the machinery of modern life. Confident that adolescence is behind them, they can now admit that their so-called sense of independence was not as fruitful as they thought it would be. They may have chosen to be popular at the risk of being unoriginal. They were prone to mistake independence for uniqueness. Now as adults, they have to guard against another temptation to pseudo-originality. To catch on to the rules of being a grown up person, they have to learn how to dress properly, to please the boss, to appear in the right places, and to socialize with influential people.

When they were adolescents, they neglected these skills, partly in protest against their parents. They lived as if they were in a different culture with rules of its own and with peer-pressured standards of success and failure. Then suddenly they were thrust into the adult world, perhaps with a family of their own that depended on their support. They had to learn the rules of how to be an adult all at once. In competition with other young adults at work and in social life, they realized their lack of skill and knowledge. To make up for this deficiency, they put out of their minds concerns for originality and ways to beat the establishment. Instead they mastered as fast as they could the ways of adult living. They feel pleased now to belong to the grown-up, practical world of young adulthood. They feel safe again, yet at times when they least expect it, they feel doubtful.

Of course, it was important for them to learn correct behavior, but is this all there is to life? As adolescents, they might have exaggerated their independence, their opposition to organizational red tape and conformity, but were they totally wrong? Did they not discover then a genuine desire to be themselves in spite of coming under the influence of other adolescents? Was there no truth to that desire? Should this experience of adolescence not be harmonized with the demands of adulthood? Maybe what they think of as being grown up refers only to mastery of the social externals of adult behavior in a competitive society while true maturity eludes them.

While they cannot deny that it was necessary to learn the ways of feeling at home in the adult world, neither can they shake the conclusion that the public seems to be satisfied with them when they conform to the externals. "You know what you have; you don't know what you will get," seems to be the favored slogan when a "public" adult advises them how to act. Now is the time to pause and remember that public adulthood is only a period of transition between adolescence and true adult life.

Why, then, do some people get stuck in this phase? Part of the reason seems to be that what was meant to be a period of training in how to live in a publicly acceptable adult manner becomes a permanent formula for how to be effective in society by "playing the game." The first rule is to conform to the patterns of propriety associated with adult life. The same pressure to excel in social conformity tends to imprison people in this period of transition. This preparatory public phase is then mistaken as an entrance to adulthood itself. It is a formidable hindrance to anyone in search of a self-motivated life. The struggle to go beyond it may require more wisdom and fortitude than that needed to leave adolescence behind. We must learn to live originally in an unoriginal world with a discerning heart that knows what demands of society we ought to accept and what we need to reject.

Once adolescents have an inkling of the horizon of meaning that lies beyond the rituals of public adulthood, they may be awakened to the fulfillment only a self-motivated life offers them. They realize that side by side with respect for original living comes a loosening of the harness of the quasi-adult life they took on rather thoughtlessly. Pure public adaptation without the complement of personal originality can never lead to appreciation of themselves and others as human beings who cannot be reduced to slavish conformity to whatever the machines of modern management want them to do. The regard they once had for the anonymous public of producers does not totally disappear, but they modify it by making a distinction between who they are and what they do. An enterprise may improve in size and profit but not at the expense of its workers. They now refuse to be anesthetized by advertising and propaganda. Self-motivated people are not the victims of the anonymous forces that move society. The public responds not to personal insights into what best fulfills us as original persons but to impersonal, often dehumanizing forces. The public media conspire to create needs designed by powerful interest groups that seldom pay attention to individual tastes and personal preferences.

As long as our adulthood remains impersonal, our daily life may be so rooted in the public mindset that we are scarcely aware of our own originality. The more moved we are by these anonymous reflexes, the more we risk not maturing as adults. The public may then hail us as meritorious, dependable citizens, who have nipped self-motivations in the bud and become proponents of impersonal complacency. True adulthood may elude us forever if we are afraid to take responsibility for our lives. In addition to not being moved from within, we may envy adults who are self-motivated; we may block their efforts to free society from excessive public-mindedness, oblivious to the fact that life in general may deteriorate because of our apathy. Lack of involvement leads to the spread of pervasive envy toward those who have become original laborers, office workers, or teachers. Fidelity to their gifts prompts them to work faster, longer, or with more dedication, but this does not mean that they will be more appreciated by their colleagues or supervisors. Adults like them threaten to awaken in others the repressed awareness of their own responsibility to embellish the role one fulfills by the deeper self one is.

It becomes impossible to know if people mean what they say when they hide behind the veil of their social roles. The higher quasi-adults climb on the ladder of their self-devised social hierarchy, the more they may be tempted to become bland instruments of public opinion, who have forfeited their originality. Techniques, projects of production and the machines that facilitate them are merely means, neutral in themselves. Their use may or may not be motivated by mature wisdom and human concern. Isolated from personal motivation, they can endanger basic human values, including the hallowed privacy of a personal life.

If we allow ourselves to be moved mainly by outside forces, we may lose touch with the loving care we ought to bring to our surroundings. Our potency for self-motivation in the social sphere may grind to a halt. Loss of inwardness leads also to distrust of our own thoughts and feelings. Even in the most sacred realms of life—like love and marriage, the education of children, and the resolution of relational conflicts—we may abide blindly by the sayings of experts. The will to be the origin of our private lives has been undercut, too. The public media offer endless reams of information and advice, supposedly to liberate us from ignorance when all that results is a new kind of bondage. We have escaped from one trap only to be ensnared by another. No wonder we are tempted to remain fixated in the transition period between adolescence and adulthood.

Another cause may be traceable to the fact that many occupations have become empty of meaning. Hours may be spent in turning out products or providing services that are useful for making a profit but may be useless for enhancing life's meaning. In these expanding bureaucratic structures, the administration of the machinery that runs them may take precedence over the women and men they were meant to serve. A truly humane society is eager to create a climate which helps people to realize their highest aspirations so that by their example the dormant originality of others may be called forth. Such a climate facilitates the transition from our being merely a public entity to being a self-motivated person.

Sound industrialization can be an avenue for liberation of originality and a lessening of envy on the condition that we do not neglect reflection on these deeper dimensions of life. Constant entertainment that purports to relieve boredom may only prolong adolescence. One may watch programs in a kind of stupor, unwilling to shut them off. This fixation on the media may also cause one to escape the enriching togetherness of family life and friendship. Televisions and computers may address our hunger for information, but they cannot squelch our longings for loving relationships with others.

The gift of friendship suffers in this climate since it presupposes that people trust one another enough to disclose their uniqueness. Young adults, having been encouraged to compete for various public roles and positions, find it difficult to let down their guard, to replace protocol with the straightforward expression of their likes and dislikes. Loneliness and the unconscious need for acceptance as a person can make them more, not less suspicious, of ever being taken seriously as adults. Replacing self-affirmation is an insatiable demand for confirmation by anyone who promises relief from the anonymity of public adulthood. The temptation to drift aimlessly from one empty relationship to another is almost impossible to resist.

Already in their family of origin, the awakening of self-motivation in children may be suppressed in favor of their becoming persons pleasing to their parents. Schools may continue the emphasis on public initiation started in the family by gearing a child's motivation towards a lucrative career. When their education in this climate comes to an end and these new adults enter the commercial world, they are likely to equate who they are with what they do. They may identify themselves with other adult roles like head of the family, golf player, social do-gooder, political demonstrator, left-winger, right-winger, middle-of-the-roader, pillar of the church, without paying much attention to their original self. Yet roles that are not made personally meaningful may deprive them of a sense of their deepest identity.

When true passion for life has been paralyzed by the machinery of society, it may feel as if there is no hope for us, but here we are mistaken. The leveling mentality may already be passing away. To reject the technical dimension of the human mind is as foolish as relying exclusively on it. Information is as necessary as formation. Both serve the disclosure of our original spirit.

The human-mind-as-spirit is meant to illumine the human-mind-as-specialist in any field of endeavor. Spontaneity of spirit should precede and accompany plans and projects proposed by technical intelligence. Each realm of knowledge facilitates our growth in spiritual originality and scientific elaboration. This partnership aids our attempts to build self-motivated lives dedicated to addressing the deepest needs of society. Help is forthcoming from every quarter of creation--from the experimental, technical, and quantitative aspects of the sciences of measurement to the experiential, reflective, and qualitative aspects of the sciences of meaning. Especially the latter encourage us to move beyond the deceptions of quasi-adulthood to the wisdom of life embedded in the experiences of enlightened adults committed to the cause of promoting social justice, peace, and mercy throughout the world. The atmosphere in which originality thrives encourages us to be original inwardly while striving to embody this originality outwardly in the pursuit of excellence in our daily tasks. Having found ourselves as original adults, we are better able to integrate public efficiency and progress with personal appreciation for the perennial values that make life worth living.

New directives beckon us to move from unoriginal to original expressions of our uniqueness, especially in this period of transition from adolescence to adulthood. Success in life comes to mean more than conformity to the demands of impersonal organizations. Compliance in the public sphere gives way to consonance with the mystery of our personal calling. The promise of higher pay does not tempt us to turn a blind eye to the needs of our family beyond the financial sphere. Experience proves that once we bind our selfhood to the functional dimension only, we may seal ourselves and others off from the higher values no amount of production and consumption can attain. To go through our days, using up our energy for material purposes but in no way fostering the joy of original living, is a formula for unhappiness. The only reward an efficient functionary may receive in the long run is an increasing dissatisfaction with the self he or she has become combined with envy of the self one could have been.

APPROACHING ADULT LIVING

We cannot deny forever the hidden call to be who we are nor can we pretend that the quest for original living can be fulfilled only by an elite few. In past eras personal growth may have been sacrificed to the growth of bureaucratic organizations, but in the present era we seem to be on the threshold of rediscovering the possibility for self-motivation—not by undermining the importance of the technological structures we have devised but by integrating them with the need to be liberated from the holding patterns of impersonal adulthood. How to accomplish this end is the challenge each of us faces. It needs to be met before the technological revolution has reached such a stage that it becomes a counter force to respect for originality and its expression in daily life. Even if this goal is reached, there is never an end to the influences that are self-alienating or to the dehumanizing forces that clamor for allegiance. We must never give up the inner effort to be ourselves amidst the clamor of public voices attempting to seduce us away from creating the conditions that facilitate personal and spiritual growth. What can we do now to overcome our envy of originality and to grow in self-motivation? Answers to this question are by no means meant to be exhaustive. They represent the beginning of a dialogue to which all of us may contribute in the coming years. The scientific and technological promises to better our lives have to be monitored by the higher motivations that make growth in respectful love—as opposed to envious disrespect—the light that guides our journey in faith and freedom.

Chapter Five
Living Originally in an Envious World

E ntering public life puts us on the precarious edge between adolescence and adulthood, between privacy and community. We start to feel the dynamic flow of presence and action that ought to characterize our adult existence. In the open-ended horizons of adolescence, it was as if the world's main purpose was to match what we wanted it to be. We were braced for change, standing at the threshold of an emerging sense of freedom. Nobody could tell us what to do. No worn out organization was worth wasting our precious time trying to preserve it. Especially while we were still in school, the pressures of society did not weigh upon us as they did on our parents and teachers. We were not yet responsible for a job or a family of our own.

The experience of stepping into an adult world changed that heady horizon of unsituated freedom. We had no choice but to face the limits placed on our fondest dreams. The sober truth dawned on us that we could go nowhere without the help of others, without the arts and disciplines afforded by a good education in academic life or other fields. It would only falsify our originality were we to live as if no one else mattered.

Young adults today must learn these lessons at a faster, more furious pace. Fearful of not making it on their own, they may sell out to the demands of a leveling society. They may give up trying to find and follow their own calling and surrender their inwardness to the fads and fashions of the day. They may displace inner responses by public reflexes and come to prefer the comfort zone of conformity to living in the creative tension between what moves them personally and what the public wants them to be.

As an adult, I can choose to affiliate with compatible social organizations, such as a union, a professional association, a leftist, rightist, or middle-of-the-road group, a sports club or a charitable enterprise. At first glance, this choice may seem to be the right one for me, but further appraisal of what it means may be necessary. Why did I join this particular group? Did I link up with such an organization because its mission statement echoed my goals or only because it seemed to advance my career? Perhaps the kind of contribution I want to make to society ties in with the aim of a company to fund low income housing but the pay scale they offer is less than I wanted to make. I silence the voice of altruism and listen only to the whisper of wealth. Activists eager to promote the cause of their choice may make me feel guilty if I do not share their enthusiasm for it. Moved by the anxious wish to look good in the public eye, I may force myself to take part in an upward career move that in due course creates a break with my true calling. I may still be committed to helping the poor in a remote way as a financial consultant, but I miss the first-hand experience of doing so.

The aim of adulthood is to maintain the dialogue between our originality and the organizations to which we belong. While fulfilling the obligations membership entails, we must monitor what we do, where we serve and with whom we associate. Involvement in social projects suitable to our calling makes us less vulnerable to give up self-motivations that arouse our awareness of cultural needs and community-mindedness. Without pausing to remember who we are, we may allow others to tell us what to do. Their social interests and ours may or may not be the same.

This example illustrates only one of the many challenges associated with living in an adult world. We must give of ourselves to others while remaining true to our given destiny. We must enter into good causes without being stymied by exalted expectations; we must live a public life but in a personal way, be a part of society without becoming alienated from our inmost originality. It is not as if our original self has to be invented by us. The essence of who we are in the mind and heart of the mystery precedes our coming into existence. Life is not a question of fabricating our destiny out of nothing but of unfolding the dispositions of the heart that are already ours.

To cultivate both patience and perseverance, we must practice the art of waiting upon the mystery in a time-conscious world that offers high praise to those who "never waste a minute." After all, by simply flicking on a switch we have instant music, light, heating, and air conditioning. By contrast, a self-motivated life cannot be forced to engage from the outside; it unfolds from within, slowly and imperceptibly, like a bud before the rose appears in full bloom.

Once a small boy received a tulip bulb as a gift from his father. He planted it in the garden behind his house. Eager to see the flower grow, he dug the bulb up many times a day. He wanted to know how its growth was progressing. It never did mature. It died before it came into the light of day.

The more we calculate original moves, the less we may succeed in finding them. Our originality has to grow, so to speak, organically in the precious soil of fidelity to the appeals emanating from our true self. We may have witnessed their birth and first blush of maturity in our family of origin. There we learned that good intentions had to be implemented in good actions like serving others in a selfless manner. The birth of these values requires an incubation period in our innermost self. They may then move outward from our original essence into the existing field of our here-and-now situation. The change from ego-to-other-centeredness does not happen automatically nor can we hasten it according to our will, no more than a flower garden can force the sun to shine and the rain to fall.

The boy who planted the bulb could not make it grow, but he could have surrounded it with fertile soil, provided it with water, exposed his plant to air and sunshine, protected it against storm, drought, and frost. By the same token, our originality needs exposure to the right values that promote it and protection from the wrong ones that paralyze it.

ORIGINALITY AND VALUE RADIATION

Sunlight encourages seeds to flower, but what awakens originality? Its nurturing ground are the values and virtues that uplift and transfigure us. We receive our originality as a gift that grows when we turn what we believe into something of benefit to others. Originality marks that depth of self where we are at once most alone and most at one with others; it is like a familiar refrain that beckons us to ponder the path we are to take to assure the quality and dignity of all human beings, ourselves included.

We may experience the motivating force of such values so personally that it feels as if we are the only ones to have lived them. Consider the awe parents feel at the birth of their first child. Countless mothers and fathers have been through this experience of pain and joy, yet in each instance it seems unrepeatable. Old as the story of love and marriage is, it is still brand new. The same orientation to what is good and true may be shared by many seekers in culture and history, but their expression of it reveals itself afresh in the attitudes they profess, in the deeds they accomplish, in the words they speak. If we are fortunate enough to live in the vicinity of self-motivated persons, the humane values we most admire may not seem so remote after all. They may touch us so profoundly that we, too, want to help others and in our own small way to make a difference in their lives.

When it comes to awakening originality, living examples are the best teachers. No amount of abstract reasoning about the values we want to embody can have the same impact on us. Values reveal their significance in action. Their efficacy shines through models and mentors it is impossible to forget. What attracts us to them has the power to evoke new directives in our own lives. These now actualized values, lived in tune with our originality, result in the growth of respect and the diminishment of envy.

Every culture is a treasure trove of centers of value radiation. Poems, plays, paintings, cathedrals, and concerts—all may speak to us of what makes life most liveable. Even in the darkest ages the world has known, no amount of tyranny could stamp out the light of faith, the beacon of hope, the lamp of love. To be touched and transformed by these embodiments of virtue, we must give up any egocentric attempt to be the captain of our ship or the master of our fate. A "what's in it for me?" attitude contrasts sharply with the witness of those who transmit to us aesthetic and altruistic values that preserve human freedom and dignity for all.

We want to read the classics because they cannot be replaced by popular texts that are here today and gone tomorrow. We do not want to lose our sensitivity to the lasting values handed on from one generation to the next. These masterpieces recorded depths of meaning still seen in the landmark creations we love today. We must guard against their loss in an informational age that equates wisdom with the whiplash of instant gratification that promises to bring us bliss but often at the price of preventing us from appropriating basic truths. Seeking short cuts to happiness turns out to be an ephemeral quest. It takes time to imbibe gifts that enhance our personhood and ensure the legacy we want to pass on to others.

ORIGINALITY AND GRATITUDE

Unlike values that last, empty promises come and go with the speed of light. To acquire them costs me little or no self-discipline or sacrifice. When I want a cup of coffee, why should I grind the beans and brew it when I can get any drink I want from a vending machine? Nothing this quick can match an encounter over coffee with a friend I have not seen for a long time, although our conversation picks up where it left off without missing a beat. Experiences like these make us smile from ear to ear; they are like a gift that keeps on giving. Sitting in a concert hall surrounded by the sound of a beautiful symphony or standing in awe before the person I love exemplify the sheer grace of original living. The opposite mentality, which threatens to reduce the journey through life to an exercise in envious comparisons, results in cutting others down to manageable size so I can impose my will on them. Since the main goal I set for myself is to get ahead of them, my relationships look like business dealings. I may try to influence possible clients by treating them to classy dinners based on the assumption that money can buy whatever I want. Then I meet a person who is not for sale, whose integrity means more to him or her than any amount of flattery. The illusion I harbored that everyone can be bought and sold, seduced and manipulated, shatters to pieces.

In the order of original living what comes first is respect for self and others, followed by the suspension of envy and the emergence of admiration. The selfish lives envious people lead cannot hold a candle to the selfless witness of those who honor their integrity and serve the common good.

ORIGINALITY AND ENVIOUS COMPARISON

The warning sign of slipping into envy flares when I perceive the values displayed by another person as a threat to my petty sense of importance. Let us say that a neighbor of mine exhibits a winning sense of style and dignity in the way she dresses, keeps her house, and landscapes her yard. She always greets people with a heart-warming smile. Whenever she participates in a neighborhood activity, she brings to her task a distinctive note of hospitality and graciousness. The meeting she chairs, the breakfast she hosts, the festivity she helps to organize go well because of her creativity. To some people she is not a *treat* to behold but a *threat* to their own standing among the neighbors. They envy her success. They cannot stand the admiration others extend to her. Their incapacity to be grateful for the gifts of their neighbor makes them respond negatively to her accomplishments.

Such envious looks may be an extension of a more general style of perception. Perhaps I have been reared to see people as products of our competitive culture. This bent toward comparative assessment begins early in life. Many of us are not taught as children to look at the gifts of others appreciatively. An envious mother may not say of another woman's child, "How wonderful Mary looks today!" or "How fast she is learning to dress herself." She feels uneasy when Mary seems to do better than her daughter Jane. This kind of comparison only becomes harmful when it descends from a genuine evaluation of what other children are like and what in them is worthy of emulation to a devaluation of their personality. The more envy escalates, the less children may be able to admire their playmates. One either has to do better than they and, if not, to belittle their gifts. In either case, envy poisons growth in respect.

Why did Jane's mother feel bad when she noticed that Mary made faster progress? When the criterion of comparison blends with the achievement mentality, it is tempting to assess others on a sliding scale of social failure or success. In a competitive society, it seems to be the yardstick by which we judge others in general.

Jane's mother in this case no longer appreciates in a detached way the worth of her own daughter. She focuses only on the success of her neighbor's child and envies her behavior. If Mary is a better learner than her Jane, she may not look like as good a mother to her neighbors. If Mary's future looks brighter than Jane's, what will others think? The grip of envious comparison begins to tighten. The feelings it evokes may influence one's entire future. Instead of looking at the unique set of virtues a person displays, we focus on how high or low they have climbed on the ladder of success. If someone has an asset that counts on this calculator, we may promote it at the price of his or her other gifts. For example, a child may show early in life a propensity for reading and reflection. He or she even likes to be alone. This character trait has nothing to do with an inability to relate to others. It may simply point to a love for books in a budding teacher. The solitude they prefer once in a while may make them seem weird to their more aggressive siblings or excitable playmates. Measured against the scale of social success, this propensity for thoughtfulness may be seen as a deficiency rather than an asset. The children in question may be prone to devalue their own gifts and to wish they were more like the other kids. When their parents point out how successful they are compared to his or her failures, the envy of others starts to take shape. Johnny feels that all would be well if only he had a different personality. Mary senses that her worth depends on how well she measures up to the standards her family sets for her. Already at an early stage, children like this may begin to strive after a life that can never be theirs. The moment they interiorize their parent's look of envious comparison, they risk becoming estranged from their true self.

We do nothing to deserve the original gifts we have been given by our Creator. Either we accept them in gratitude or we make them into objects of envious comparison. The demise of gratitude marks the birth of envy as a leveling force. Comparing ourselves with others blinds us to the gifts with which we have been endowed. More than social success, which we may or may not enjoy, they grant us a far more lasting set of dispositions rooted in a grateful heart. To make comparative assessments the basis of our happiness is precarious. We are always in danger of meeting people who are better off socially than we are. If we build our worth merely on what others determine to be the only standard of success, we are bound to feel a twinge of envy every time we meet people more eminent than ourselves.

The factors that determine social success can change from one day to the next. A short while ago folks with a facility for setting up their own business enjoyed prominence in society. With the coming of the era of large corporations, factory work seemed preferable to running a "mom and pop supermarket." The praise once bestowed on small business owners was now extended to manufacturing agents. This historical sensitivity to the up-and-down meaning of success can ameliorate the danger of one group of workers envying another. The habit of envious comparison is hard to break. Rather than focusing on what we can contribute to society in as unique a way as possible, we analyze who has more or less talent in what field. That schools may be breeding places for envy ought not to surprise us. The values of the society for which workers must be prepared invade their hallowed halls. The marketplace of consumerism plays on the dynamics of envy to sell goods and services to customers who "would die" to be better off than their peers. The productive society uses envy to incite people to work harder for the acquisition of higher positions that prove, at least in their mind, that the more one exerts oneself the bigger will be one's reward.

This habit of comparison fuels the fires of envy already burning in family life, school, and society. Success based on envious tactics will always find room to promote comparative, often cutthroat competition. Such deformative dispositions must be plucked from our spirit like weeks in a garden. Otherwise they may entrench themselves in our character and personality, eroding the original gifts we have been given in accordance with our call. What one measures oneself against are the skills, rewards, and remunerations given to others independent of one's own originality. Education becomes a test of how well one has mastered certain subjects useful in society. The love of learning is secondary to the career-oriented success one achieves or misses. One's guiding light is not the gift one is but the amount of money one has.

GRATITUDE FOR VALUES IN OTHERS

Living in a spirit of gratitude enables us to accept with humility the undeserved gifts we and others have received. We do not own our originality in the same way as we possess a bicycle, a new car, a bookcase, or a French poodle. What distinguishes us is our ability to appreciate the manifestation of virtue in our own and others' lives. Their goodness may be so radiant that they become for us an appeal to incarnate the same lights in our own life. We resonate with the service orientation they set. We see in them the respectful presence to one's original calling we want to make our own.

This appeal to uniqueness decreases the summons to copy blindly another person's life. It points to a higher realm of values like the ones that motivated men as different as Abraham Lincoln and Albert Einstein. Despite character flaws that are inevitable in anyone's personality, they exhibited a love for humanity and a quest for truth admired by all. They heard and heeded the summons to nobility hidden in every soul. These historical figures and the originality they represent heighten our hopes of resisting the distorting mirrors of envious comparison and awakening instead to the clarity of our call.

DWELLING AND ORIGINAL LIVING

Original living freed from envy is gracious, non-comparative, and full of respect. It encourages the *disposition of dwelling* by which we allow ourselves to be present to reality as it is. When I dwell in the woods, my mood is different than when I drive on a super highway. Life ought to be that way. Instead of switching from one lane to the next, I need to attend to where I am and then decide where I need to go and how to get there. I feel relaxed and focused in a way that is not possible when I have to fight my way through traffic to reach my office on time. When I abide in awe-filled attention, I become more aware of the meanings I miss in the hectic round of an overly scheduled life.

I smell with delight flowers freshly in bloom. I look in wonder at swans floating on a lake that shimmers in the morning light. A beautiful young doe may captivate my attention for a superb moment as she stands in perfect stillness among firs and evergreens. I catch my breath as she turns and leaps away in graceful agility.

Moments like these are by merely functional standards impractical. My perceptions, thoughts, and feelings seem to leave their well-trodden ways. I experience anew the richness of the ordinary. I begin to ask questions I may not ponder during working hours. This dwelling posture draws me into realms of self-awareness and creativity I may not have entered previously.

A contemporary example of the link between dwelling and originality can be seen in the so-called "Laboratory Theater" started by Jerry Grotowski in 1959. Eight unknown actors and this young director of only twenty-six came together to form a company in a provincial town in Poland. One of the distinctive features of this experimental theater was its interest in bringing new life to classical dramas, poems, plays, myths, and parables. Director and actors dwelt on the hidden depths of meaning conveyed in this literature. They assimilated it personally. They experienced theatrical works in a way that was both timely and timeless. The cast tried to express as honestly as they could what they felt while abiding with these dramatists of the past. Grotowski wanted them not so much to memorize the scripts as to confront them. They were instructed to disclose their universal meaning by abiding with them. The actors were to participate so respectfully in the living words of the author that they became their own. Only then could they convey an age-old message to present-day audiences. Through constant dwelling, the text came to life in the actors even when they abandoned on stage many external props. Grotowski's actors might be poor in the theatrical sense, but they were rich in their ability to imbibe and impersonate the original insights the playwright intended to convey across the ages. In this way, actors and audiences gave voice to the original experiences of our common humanity.

The average person may not be able to recreate these masterpieces as impressively as an artist does, but he or she can assimilate and embody them uniquely. Such monuments of humankind's experience are not bound to one or the other culture. One does not have to live with the ancients to appreciate the experiences described by Homer in the *Iliad* and the *Odyssey*. Universal human moments of truth may be expressed by composers, sculptors, painters, poets, philosophers, and spiritual masters. The music of Bach, Beethoven, and Mozart can thrill Eastern listeners as much as Japanese *Noh* plays can inspire Western viewers. Their compositions reverberate at such depths of human longing that they touch audiences everywhere. The peaks and valleys of life they have dwelt upon and expressed in an artistic manner never lose their validity.

Here again the paradox of originality confronts us: when we are most alone, we are most together. Solitude is the partner of solidarity. In spite of our differences, it feels as if we know one another. We manifest uniquely the human traits we all share. This point again proves that originality goes beyond the inventiveness of those gifted to shape new cultural forms. Homer's works are immortal not because he invented new ways of using language but because he combined with his creative genius for poetry the power to convey the joys and sorrows all of us experience.

WONDER AND CURIOSITY

At the heart of dwelling is a mood of wonder that differs from the curiosity that stands behind scientific and practical enterprises. If the question "What works?" is the only one we ask, it may lead to the death of our sense of wonder. Children awaken to wonder by hearing fairy tales and reciting catchy rhymes. These imaginative flights allow them to experience life poetically before they attempt to organize it practically.

When we meet life in wonder and respect, we admire what is there without having to master it. Wonder evokes originality and weakens envy. It helps us to keep our ambitions in check, thereby lessening the risk that functionalism cancel our capacity for transcendence. Wonder connotes a readiness on our part to abide with any value worthy of our consideration. Curiosity embellishes information; wonder sustains spiritual formation. Curiosity causes us to move from point to point until a problem is solved; wonder allows room for the mystery at the center of our life; it enables us to live more fully in the moment what we feel in our heart. It adds a new layer of understanding and experience to the original way in which we fulfill our daily tasks.

The Anatomy Lesson of Doctor Tulp is a famous painting by Rembrandt, who had seen medical students and professors dissecting cadavers and wanted to depict these men at work. Curiosity about human anatomy makes us look with interest at this masterpiece, but only wonder enables us to absorb its presentation of the mystery of death and the sacredness of life.

In the same vein a moment of awesome wonder transcends the arrogance that motivates avid curiosity. Wonder is not about what we can measure by comparisons, tests, and questionnaires; it lingers like the scent of a lovely perfume long after our curiosity about its brand name has been satisfied. It lets us sense values whose meaning we can never exhaust. It accompanies every expression of genuine love and holds in check the harmful tendency to label persons and file them away.

As controllers of the biosocial conditions of our lives, we revel in scientific and practical curiosity; we engage in an endless search for more relevant information about our environment, but we must not do so at the expense of killing wonder. The satisfaction of our curiosity gives us a semblance of dominion over others and the world. The details we assemble may create the illusion of control, but this disposition has to be tempered by more reverent concerns.

An accomplished educator strives to inform her students as well as to inspire them. She knows it is beyond her to compel an original experience or to arouse wonder at will. She aims instead to foster an abiding approach that opens her students both to the wisdom of the past and the challenges of the present. She hopes to awaken them to an awareness of their own capacity for creativity.

Education to wonder and education to curiosity are both necessary. The former encourages us to dwell on the original values and meanings we share with humanity. The latter enables us to keep informed about matters that enhance our knowledge of universe and history while reminding us that what we know never exhausts the vastness of what we have yet to learn.

CLOSED OR OPEN CURIOSITY

Curiosity that diminishes our sense of wonder may become so absorbing that it leaves no room for abiding in awe-filled attention. Whereas this kind of closed curiosity presumes to master the mystery, open curiosity respects the information we obtain while acknowledging its limited value. If we foster closed curiosity only, it may lead us to believe that sciences of measurement are sufficient to disclose all we need to know about life. The sense of wonder that ought to complement our search for truth in the light of sciences of meaning may be subdued almost to the point of extinction.

Our present-day culture holds the informational approach in the highest regard. Collections of scientific data purport to represent all there is to know, whether with exactitude or a residue of uncertainty. This belief in closed curiosity as an end in itself proves to be self-defeating when, despite our best efforts, we are still confronted by the infinite reaches of time and eternity. Open curiosity leaves room for wonder and lets us see that scientific knowledge is not an end in itself but a means to enhance our quest for truth and our encounters with a mystery beyond any semblance of human mastery. Simply because we have the tools to do something may or may not mean that we ought to proceed prior to discerning right from wrong.

Open curiosity fosters research while reminding us that its fruits are relative in comparison to all that escapes what the human mind can know. It does not diminish information-gathering, but neither does it confine its conclusions to only measurable results. Open curiosity does not lessen inquisitiveness; it quiets the impetuousness that tends to make informational thinking absolute to the exclusion of the mystery.

CONVENTIONS OF SOCIETY AND ORIGINALITY

Two other dynamics of original living need to complement one another: the first is to follow the conventions of society in a reasonable way; the second is to personalize them by the use of our unique gifts and talents. Consider what happens when we learn how to write. We follow the lessons taught to all beginners like how to hold a pen and slant our paper, but before long our writing style begins to show personal features. Our script, as handwriting experts believe, can even shed light on our personality. Perhaps we write in a mechanical way, imitating for a lifetime the models given to us in elementary school. Who we are does not shine through in our penmanship. It is as if we have sacrificed what is original about our writing to conform to what is conventional.

Any practice can serve to withhold or release the emergence of our selfhood. The customs of our culture can hamper originality or enhance it. Take the simple example of a handshake. Over the course of time people had to find a quick way to assure one another that they could be trusted. They did so by showing an open hand. Each one could see that no weapon was concealed. Soon the offering of an open hand came to symbolize a basically trustworthy exchange. This custom led to our familiar mode of handshaking as a way for one person to express interest in another. By the same token, due to our differences, handshakes may be stiff or cordial, comforting or confrontational.

Conventions remain dead routines as long as we do not enliven them with our originality. Once dead customs should not be expected to come to life overnight. Some may be so far removed from our present-day experiences that they cannot be restored at all. Our only choice in that case is to invent better customs to be lived by people in their own way.

COMMON SENSE AND ORIGINAL WISDOM

Originality exacts a promise on our part to accept personal responsibility for our actions. In every situation we face, we need to ask: "What must I do to remain faithful to who I am?" The conventional customs of the different groups to which we belong may guide our response in part, but they tend to be rather general. Often they tell us only what we should not do to behave like a civilized person. The question remains: "What ought I to do as the unique person I am?" For example, given my temperament and background, what response should I make to a person who tries to take advantage of my kindness and pokes fun at my politeness? In situations such as this, how can I remain polite without repressing my originality?

A first condition for exercising original wisdom is insight: "What does it mean for me to be my best self individually while serving others in my surroundings? "Insight tells me which customs of my culture need to be adopted and which rejected to achieve my goals in the working places of family, church, and society. Among them, one could name comradeship, respect, gratitude, graciousness, admiration, compassion, and truthfulness. Enlightened by insight and common sense, I learn to act in tune with my originality on a human and a cultural level.

Consider the case of a research scientist in biochemistry whom I met on campus. He was a hard worker despite his own precarious health problems. Being a kind-hearted soul he took note of how the homeless in our city suffered from malnutrition. He accepted the invitation to volunteer as part of a team to distribute food to them several days a week and to relieve their loneliness with a friendly word. Not long thereafter he sensed that the charitable tasks he had volunteered to do combined with his need for rest greatly diminished the time, energy, and attention he needed in the laboratory. There he began to examine the effects of chronic malnutrition on one's whole metabolism. His dream was to discover potent nutrients that could be mass-produced as economically as possible—a discovery that would be of help not only for the underfed in our city but also for countless malnourished people throughout the world. The questions he asked himself were: "Should I continue my involvement with these local services with their impact on my research or would it be best for me to forgo direct food distribution to the poor and serve them indirectly by finding a scientific solution to the problem of malnutrition? Should I confine myself to my laboratory and run the risk of being called an ivory-tower scientist or should I still engage in this volunteer effort but only on a monthly basis?"

General counsels like "Be charitable" do not give us the concrete answers we need in the actual situations where we live and work. They only offer us an overall orientation as to what we ought to do, but it is up to us to decide the exact course of action to take in the situation itself. This decision leads us to consider our original calling, our personal assets, and our concern for others. Armed with such self-knowledge, we are able to meet our moment by moment obligations without neglecting the subtle dictates of our originality.

The acquisition of unique insight does not mean that we have to reinvent the generally accepted principles of conventional wisdom. Originality presupposes these universals and helps us to actualize them in daily life. It takes its departure from the given situation and seeks the proper response. For instance, what ought a teacher to do in regard to a student who once applied himself to his courses but now acts obstreperously to impress his peers? The student's emotional opposition to the voices of authority lowers his powers of concentration. The teacher tries to change his behavior as gently and firmly as possible. Myriad factors have to be considered in dialogue with the situation in which she finds herself. Her original humanity cannot be forfeited in anger; it has to be expressed in the consistent manner in which she carries out wise decisions for her own and her student's benefit.

Such insights must be reinforced by loving respect for who I am without in any way violating the rights of others. On the contrary, care for them is part of my call. The teacher in question remained faithful to who she was by maintaining a balance between her authoritative position and her compassion. Her need to care and her embodiment of this virtue in her unique style of service were fruitful expressions of her original being.

The connection between common sense and original wisdom has to be operative in the context of my handling complex challenges like how to admonish someone without overly offending them. Say an acquaintance asks me to drive him home and I am able and free to do so. I respond to this request without much thought as I do to many other uncomplicated incidences of everyday life. Original discretion is at work, but it does not need to be in high gear.

The scene changes when I see that the person who asks me for a ride is a cunning operator who tries to impose his companionship on me so that he may use it for his own purposes. His manipulative style of advancement is so at odds with what I believe that I have to become a "master of suspicion." I do not want to be used by him, but neither do I want to unstitch our acquaintanceship too quickly lest he accuse me of being an uncaring person. If I appear too often with him, others may conclude that we are special friends. Yet I do not want to hurt his feelings unnecessarily. Shall I drive him home again today? What will we talk about if I do so? How can I convey the message that this ride is an exception, not a custom? In this complicated case, there is no quick response. Original wisdom, insight, and discretion have to operate in tandem. I must weigh all aspects of the matter and act deliberately.

Thankfully, such agonizing appraisals are not necessary prior to every decision we make. Often the elements of common sense play their role so quickly that they remain unnoticed and appraisal proceeds with lightning speed. A situation ought not to be given more attention than necessary. It is unwise to tax our original resources to the point of becoming so anxious and vigilant that we cannot enjoy a moment of relaxation. This process can proceed so quickly because guiding me are many previous appraisals of the same nature, made in similar situations. I have formed a pattern of self-motivations that keeps me faithful to my originality in a variety of encounters. Many that I now face are in line with those I have confronted in the past. I do not have to start over again each time a choice presents itself because I am accustomed to following my call and not a series of self-defeating compromises.

Original appraisals built up over the years offer us a stock of knowledge upon which to draw in relation to both arduous and enjoyable tasks. All of life—from solitary reflection to conversations with good company—awakens new facets of our originality. To be guarded against is the deterioration of common sense into trite slogans that leave no room for personal appraisals in tune with my originality. I may find myself surrounded by countless experts, each with their own arsenal of advice. Self-help books bombard me with minute admonitions about every detail of life. I must be wise enough to take their suggestions into account without allowing them to take over the wisdom I have accumulated through insight and experience.

In the unique situation where providence places us, we are the experts responsible for our actions. We can never abandon our responsibility to the guidance of pundits or the public, especially when we are on the verge of making a decision that will shape our future. Respectfully assessing the advice of trustworthy others is part of the process, but we have to be willing to stand alone or else our life may not be ours. We will have lost our powers of original wisdom and discretion by allowing "what they say" to take precedence over what we know to be true.

FLEXIBLE RESPONSES OR INFLEXIBLE REACTIONS

When we try to live originally in an unoriginal world, we may become aware of an opposite tendency in us, one that interferes with the flexibility of self-motivation. Despite our best efforts, we may still experience the power of a coercive security directive that compels us to please others more than to listen to our own heart. Such coercions make us doubt our own inmost motivations. Instead of responding to a situation, we repeat certain reactions no matter how ill adapted they may be. Blind compliance blocks the flow of a self-motivated life. We say something rash or come to a quick conclusion we live to regret. Both reactions are out of touch with the real problems with which we must cope. At their root may be childhood deformations we've never quite resolved. Raised in a house of angry people, we felt overwhelmed by the fear of saying anything that might provoke more rage in those around us. These sentiments compelled us to react in a manner that was increasingly inappropriate. Our way of defying our parents may have led to thoughtless rebellion one minute and cowardly submissiveness the next. In either case, we reacted to the situation without an adequate response. Instead of being flexible and fair, we were prone to cling fanatically to one opinion, expression, or pattern of behavior. Failing to listen to reason, we became a pawn of old coercions dictated by anger. It is as if we had frozen our original self and refused to let it be thawed out by the reality of a responsive appraisal of every situation.

These powerful feelings and the reactions or responses to which they give rise are not readily available to our focal consciousness. The only sign of their appearance for better or worse is the behavior that follows. Inexplicably we may find ourselves spouting angry denunciations or tightening our fists in stubborn resistance. Our tone becomes absolute; we keep insisting on a point, driving it home relentlessly. We are unable to remain sensitive to the feelings of others. A kind of obsession keeps us captive of this urge to violent repetition of the same opinion.

When we feel these one-sided reactions welling up, we may be tempted to say: "That's typical of me; it's too bad, but people should take me as I am." Is this the real me or is it a tenacious remnant of an infantile response neither understood nor digested by me as a child? Doing my own thing is frequently mistaken as expressing my original self.

Maturation in our personal and spiritual life rests on the discovery and resolution of these compulsive drives. Once we begin to live with more ease, we may recognize when and why we lose our relaxed sense of self and resort to coercive reactions. We need to identify what gives rise to these feelings and why they take away our freedom. We may then be able to locate the coercions that bring on this behavior. As soon as we detect what triggers it, we can reflect on it and ask ourselves what are the hidden feelings behind it. We may then muster the courage to look into our history and try to remember how and when similar reactions gained a foothold in our character. While it may not be possible to uncover the exact childhood incident that is at the root of our rigidity, we need to bring to light the compulsive conduct that accounts for this unsavory effect. We cannot put all the blame on our childhood, *but* a closer look at its deformations may explain some of the problems that present themselves on a regular basis.

As our self-understanding increases, the hold of infantile compulsions on our life may diminish. Self-motivations may take the place of coercive security directives. In some cases, the hold of the past may be so strong that we really need to seek professional help. The power of such reactions is the greatest challenge we face in our search for an original life since their strength comes from a time in the past when they eluded conscious awareness.

Another force that inhibits original unfolding concerns the cultural directives communicated to us at a phase of life following childhood. So convincing may they be that we go along with them like branches flowing aimlessly down the river. We are so identified with our culture that we do not realize how much its directives hamper our self-unfolding. Without growth in original wisdom, these cultural dictates often crush uniqueness, promote envy of originality, and prevent us from living a self-motivated life.

One view upheld by a culture caught in the compulsion to be current may be that its conclusions overshadow totally the wisdom of faith and formation traditions tested in the past. To question popular norms is to be dubbed naive. The high premium society places on the practical, functional, and scientific aspects of life may draw some people to conclude that subduing nature for productive purposes is more important than protecting our planet. Past wisdom spoke to us of a time to sow seeds and a time to harvest their bounty. Life was interwoven with the myths of birth and death; it was not reduced to building a set of skills to tame the universe. Original living refuses to sever itself from the foundational truths that lie at the heart of any humane civilization.

One suggestion to safeguard our commitment to pass essential values on to the next generation may be to foster the emergence of centers of value-radiation. Here people can be given the time and freedom they need to uphold the value of scientific endeavors as well as the arts and disciplines conducive to religious presence. The vitality of the culture as a whole is not necessarily present at any one moment. Values neglected in one phase of history must be protected so that they can reassert themselves at a later period.

Centers representative of less popular values may exert less influence at this time, but their radiation power, though dimmed, lies in wait for another day. What strikes us as paradoxical is the fact that it is not the popular but the unpopular centers of value-radiation that are crucial for the maintenance and unfolding of a culture. Values that are highly lauded in a specific phase of cultural development take care of themselves, as it were. Functionality may be lived and articulated enthusiastically during a given cultural period, but its one-sided emphasis cannot last. Sooner or later a hunger for the transcendent presents itself. That is why the concern expressed in religious centers of value-radiation often centers on forgotten values that for a while may be unpopular and neglected but do not go away.

The problem is that characters obsessed by envy may try to silence the lonely prophets destined to uphold these values for all people. They refuse to believe that sooner or later the historical situation that temporarily underestimated these values will change. Then its original witnesses may be recognized with gratitude, partly because of genuine interest in its preservation and partly because new concerns have rekindled a need this and future generations can no longer deny.

CULTURAL VALUES AND ORIGINAL VIEWS

A civilization could be carried away by the one-sidedness characteristic of a cultural period. It may try to deceive us into believing that our affinity for such values is a farce, but we know the opposite is true. Without adherence to these values, we cannot remain true to our calling. Self-alienation might lead to forgetfulness of our uniqueness and the value-radiation it implies. We might forfeit the joy of original living and adopt a routinized direction that is not fulfilling. That is why throughout this book I have tried to encourage everyone to be their original self despite the danger of evoking envy. To stand for the forgotten values of humanity in a specific cultural period is a noble duty since any kind of one-sidedness poses a threat to our survival. A temporarily dismissed center devoted to protecting and preserving threatened values may no longer attract great numbers in its defense, but this lack of popularity in no way affects its importance. What matters most is that we remain faithful to the call we feel to live originally in an often dangerously envious, unoriginal world.

Made in the USA
Lexington, KY
09 December 2012